STUDENT PORTFOLIOS

A Learning Tool

Phyllis Lightfoot

Pat Davidson

ACKNOWLEDGEMENTS

To Heather Ast, Cora Gaillard, Angie Musyj, and Lori Parada.

For piloting the portfolio process and providing valuable input and students examples.

To Nicole Person.

For sharing your knowledge and expertise of the portfolio process as well as contributions of student and parent reflections.

To the many students and parents who contributed self-reflections, quotations, and response sheets.

To Mary-Anne Neal.

For your support and encouragement.

Table of Contents

Preface

In its pledge to prepare our youth for a twenty-first century workforce and way of life, educators are looking at ways to ensure that goals and learning outcomes reflect a changing world. In our information age society, individuals require knowledge, skills, and competencies to access, understand, and analyze information for problem solving and decision-making situations. Curriculum, instruction, and assessment practices, therefore, must reflect a student-centered approach. This means empowering students to become responsible for their own learning in preparation for continuous growth and development of knowledge beyond their school-based years.

In recognizing the education system's responsibility in preparing today's students to be successful and productive citizens in a global world, provinces and states are implementing portfolios as part of their graduation requirements. In British Columbia, for example, the Ministry of Education has set in place the *Graduation Portfolio Program.* This is a three-year process that provides students with the framework to set their own educational and career course. Students gather evidence of skills, knowledge, and attitudes based on program requirements and options throughout grades 10, 11, and 12. Portfolio guidelines center around skills and proficiencies associated with areas such as career planning, employability skills, information technology, and personal health. More importantly, graduation portfolios will "evolve into a unique expression of the students' interests, abilities, and goals" (British Columbia Ministry of Education, 2005, p. 3).

Elementary, middle, and junior secondary schools serve to provide a foundation of skills for this portfolio process. Additionally, portfolio assessment in itself is receiving acclamation from research and literature sources as an effective and efficient authentic assessment tool to enhance the teaching and learning process. Students become actively engaged in assessment by reflecting on their own learning to monitor progress and set goals for improvement. Teachers become facilitators to guide students as the story of their learning unfolds.

Student Portfolios: A Learning Tool is designed to provide teachers with a practical handbook to implement the portfolio assessment process. It presents information in a teacher-friendly manner with instructional strategies, lesson plan ideas, and web sites to support classroom practices. The manual will guide teachers from the first activity of introducing portfolios to students, all the way through to the self-reflection and sharing stages. Teachers, who have piloted this handbook, as well as students and parents, provide their thoughts and insights on the various stages of portfolio assessment. Above all, the handbook ensures a smooth and successful transition for students as they complete graduation portfolio programs and prepare to become responsible members of their communities.

Section I: Assessment and the Portfolio Process

Today's educators went through the school system at a time when assessment *of* learning prevailed as the means to determine a student's achievement of standards or learning outcomes. This consisted of classroom, school, district, and provincial or state exams in which standardized results were used to evaluate the status of a student's progress. Current research and subsequent learning theories and principles support the use of multiple assessments to acquire an accurate and holistic profile of student learning and achievement. As such, alternative assessment practices need to become part of a school's assessment system. "Assessment information should be used to adapt instruction to meet student needs" (Leahy, Lyon, Thompson, & William, 2005, p. 22). In order for change and improvement in assessment methods to take place, educators must first change their paradigm, or mindset. To assist in this endeavor, a general discussion of assessment and the learning process follows.

Assessment and Evaluation

Assessment and evaluation are two interrelated processes that serve to facilitate learning and achievement. The British Columbia (BC) Ministry of Education (1999) defines assessment as "the systematic gathering of information about what students know, are able to do, and are working toward" (¶ 2). Common assessment practices include performance standards and rubrics, curriculum-based measurements, self-evaluations, work sampling, quizzes and tests, observations, check lists, conferences, and portfolios. Evaluation is described as follows:

> Student performance is evaluated from the information collected through assessment activities. Teachers use their insight, knowledge about learning, and experience with students, along with the specific criteria they establish, to make judgments about student performance in relation to prescribed learning outcomes. (¶ 3)

Student Self-Reflection

Name: Graison
Date: October 25

Work Sample: My math quiz

I am proud of this entry that I chose for my portfolio because:

I got 87 out of 88. I tried to be focused so I could learn the math work.

Some new things that I learned are:

I learned to stay on task.

I learned how to work hard.

Signature: Graison

Grade 2 Work Sample

As an example of assessment and evaluation, consider the *BC Performance Standards*. These documents provide an *assessment* method that integrates prescribed learning outcomes with performance-based standards. Data from the performance standards serves to *evaluate* student progress in the following ways: identify students who may benefit from intervention; develop a profile of a class or group of students to support instructional decision-making; and collaboratively set goals for individuals, classes, or schools (British Columbia [BC] Ministry of Education, 2000). Essentially, assessment is the process of gathering data; evaluation is the process of using this information to make judgments and decisions regarding student performance, progress, and program needs.

A variety of assessment practices will provide an accurate and comprehensive profile of student growth and development. Literature sources refer to assessment as revealing a *story* of student learning. In this light, "*it is essential that each contributing assessment provide dependable information* about the part of the story it is intended to represent" (Stiggins, 2001, p. 472). The assessment method should be appropriate to the task, and the student's stage of learning in order to provide a reliable foundation for judgment, decision, and amendments of judgment (BC Primary Teachers' Association, 1992). To accomplish such a feat, authentic assessment practices need to be incorporated into children's learning experiences.

Authentic Assessment

"To accurately evaluate what a person has learned, an assessment method must examine his or her collective abilities. This is what is meant by authentic assessment" ("Authentic Assessment," n.d., ¶ 1).

Inherent to authentic assessment is that a student's learning profile is established through meaningful and real life applications of learning, rather than traditional methods such as test results. Authentic assessments focus on students' performances to enable them to "demonstrate their knowledge, skills, or competencies in whatever way they find appropriate" (¶ 5). Common authentic assessment techniques

For more information on *Assessment and Evaluation* and *Criterion-Referenced Evaluation*, visit the following page at the British Columbia Ministry of Education web site: http://www.bced.gov.bc.ca/irp/pp/ppapd intro.htm

The ministry also offers an Assessment Handbook Series consisting of the following titles: *Performance Assessment, Portfolio Assessment, Student-Centered Conferences,* and *Student Self-Assessment.* For descriptions of the handbooks and ordering information, visit http://www.bced.gov.bc.ca/classroom_ assessment/abouthand.htm

"As teachers, we use observation charts, checklists, anecdotal records, reading inventories, discussions, student goal setting and action planning, as well as student, teacher and peer conferences. These can all be added to student portfolios."

Heather Ast, Grade 4 Teacher

include performance standards, portfolios, rubrics, checklists, observations, and conferences.

The task ahead for educators is to promote such authentic assessment practices to involve students, provide for a variety of learning needs, and encompass individual and peer learning experiences. This belief is in line with assessment *for* learning, which emphasizes utilizing assessment to enhance the learning and teaching process. Stiggins (2002) outlines important principles in order for assessment for learning to be effective: informing students of learning goals, setting criteria for assignments, developing assessment exercises and scoring procedures that accurately reflect student achievement, providing descriptive feedback to guide improvement, continuously revising instruction as reflected from classroom assessments, and engaging students in regular self-assessment to identify their strengths and weaknesses. Assessment for learning methods provides a framework for students to keep learning and build their level of confidence in their capabilities to become ultimately responsible for their own learning.

Portfolios as an Authentic Assessment Tool

The BC Ministry of Education (1994) describes portfolio assessment as follows:

> Portfolio assessment is a method of gathering student work samples for the purpose of evaluating student knowledge and learning. The process includes student participation in the selection of work, in criteria and goal setting, and through self-assessment. Students and teachers collaborate in assessing and evaluating student learning from evidence in the portfolio collection, then use this information to make plans and set goals for further learning. (p. 1)

Student work samples serve as *evidence* of student learning and progress. Portfolios are considered authentic assessment since the work captures students' meaningful application of their knowledge and skills (Mueller, 2003a) as well as providing an "ongoing documentation and evaluation process

For concise and useful information on all aspects of assessment, visit the following page at the *North Central Regional Educational Laboratory* web site: http://www.ncrel.org/sdrs/issues.htm and the *Funderstanding* web site at: http://www.funderstanding.com/assessment.cfm

To view an informative portfolio web site, peruse Jon Mueller's *Authentic Assessment Toolbox* at http://jonathan.mueller.faculty.noctrl.edu/toolbox/porfolios.htm

designed to improve the teacher's instructional practices and student learning" (Meisels, 1997, p. 1).

The processes that are required to create a portfolio contribute to valuable learning experiences. Consider the example of the writing process. It is the process that provides the means for students to produce a successful writing piece as well as apply it to all writing activities, an important aspect of lifelong learning. Such processes promote the development of valuable skills. As the BC Ministry of Education (2004) describes, portfolio experiences benefit students by encouraging them to become more aware of their learning, act and reflect, set goals and make decisions, and practice self-evaluation. Additionally, students are also presented with opportunities to think critically, solve problems, develop creativity, apply learning strategies, and value learning (2004). By providing explicit instruction, guidance, and practice with the process, students become empowered to initiate and complete a successful product independently.

Metacognition and the Portfolio Process

"People's knowledge of their own learning and cognitive processes and their consequent regulation of those processes to enhance learning and memory are collectively known as metacognition" (University of Phoenix, 2002, p. 362).

Simply stated, metacognition involves learning how to learn best. For example, a metacognitive skill for students to monitor comprehension is to ask themselves questions as they read or to summarize passages of the text. Literature sources state that "the more metacognitively sophisticated students are, the higher their school learning and achievement are likely to be" (as cited in University of Phoenix, 2002, p. 362). By documenting and reflecting on growth and development through the portfolio process, students analyze, facilitate, and monitor their own learning. This entails identifying strengths and weaknesses, examining efforts that lead to improvement, determining features for achieving success, and understanding effective strategies that contribute to acquiring knowledge and skills.

"You definitely need that one-on-one time with each student, especially at the grade one level, to properly teach them to set realistic goals and practice self-reflection."

Angie Musyj, Grade I Teacher

Section II:
The Portfolio Process: Getting Started

Scrapbooks: A Place to Begin

Many teachers, particularly of primary grades, use scrapbooks to collect and illustrate student work. Scrapbooks are often displayed at student-led conferences and open house events, then sent home in June as an anthology and/or keepsake of the school year. Scrapbook contents usually include a variety of student materials such as work samples from core subjects, artwork, photos, and recognition certificates or awards. By implementing some basic elements, teachers can transform the scrapbook concept into portfolio assessment.

As is the case with any assessment, it is the quality of the portfolio process that will reveal an accurate representation of student progress and achievement. To ensure the reliability of portfolio assessment, key components should include the following: establishing the overall purpose, selecting the type of portfolio, considering the audience, designing the criteria and selection process, determining the time frame, and generating and/or choosing self-reflection activities (Mueller, 2003a; Rolheiser, Bower, & Stevahn, 2000). These are interrelated in that choices regarding one aspect will influence decisions about the other elements (see Figure 1).

Figure 1. Key elements of the portfolio process.

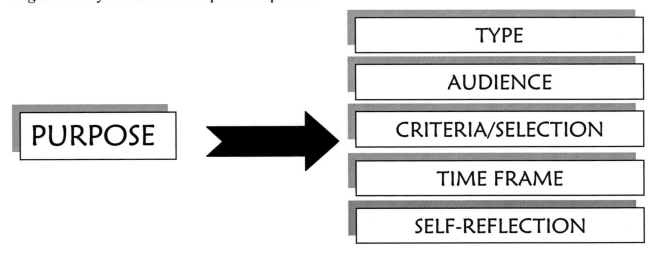

Purpose and Type of Portfolios

All of the decisions regarding the portfolio stem from the purpose (Frank, 1995). "The kind of portfolio...what goes in it...how and why and how often things are selected...what you do with it...how it's shared...all depend on why you're doing" (p. 164) a portfolio.

As with scrapbooks, the purpose of portfolios is often to highlight best, favourite, or most meaningful work. In this case, the purpose of developing a portfolio is synonymous with the type of portfolio. Such titles include *Best Work Portfolio*, *The Celebration Portfolio*, or *Showcase Portfolios*. As Stiggins (2001) states, "this is a wonderful place for young students to begin their portfolio development experience by just collecting favourite pieces of work" (p. 474).

Growth portfolios demonstrate a student's development and growth over time (Rolheiser et al., 2000). "Development can be focused on academic or thinking skills, content knowledge, self-knowledge, or any area that is important in your setting" (p. 4). Common contents of growth portfolios include drafts and final copies of writing, early and later pieces of work, and pre and post-test scores (e.g., spelling and math basic facts). Such concrete documentation of change and growth represents progress toward achieving learning outcomes or standards. This constitutes a significant accountability factor as this evidence of learning and achievement can be shared with parents during reporting periods and other staff members associated with a student's educational program. As an example of a reading and writing growth portfolio that spans kindergarten through grade two, visit <http://dp.ideasconsulting.com/dp/colleen/index.html>.

Consistent assessments will establish valid and reliable performance results for the growth portfolio. For example, the BC writing performance standards include quick scales, or rubrics, that list specific criteria based on four aspects of writing: meaning, style, form, and conventions. Including performance standards with writing pieces throughout the year will enable students to observe their progress of specific skills (e.g., sentence structure, punctuation, grammar, organization, etc.). Additionally, using the same assessment for all writing activities ensures an accurate representation of

"Portfolios really help me to introduce appropriate language associated with subject areas such as reading and writing (e.g., using terminology such as reading for meaning, reading with fluency, writing with a voice, using descriptive words, etc.). We develop language together that we both (students and teacher) understand and, as a team, use it to support our learning."

Nicole Person, Grade 2 Teacher

"You see tremendous growth in reading and writing in grade one. It's exciting when students see their growth through portfolio reflections."

Angie Musyj, Grade I Teacher

Access the BC Performance Standards for key areas of learning at this BC Ministry of Education web page: http://www.bced.gov.bc.ca/perf_stand s/.

student progress that, in effect, will guide instructional decisions to improve and promote learning. In effect, precise assessment will direct appropriate and meaningful evaluation.

Reading fluency probes and running records provide tangible evidence of student growth. By including reading samples each term with a calculation of word recognition accuracy, students observe their progress and accomplishments over time. Charting or graphing data engages students in documenting their own progress to reflect on their learning journey.

KWL charts make a valuable contribution to growth portfolios. Progress becomes apparent to students as they record their newfound knowledge and compare it to the pre-learning stage. Such experiences encourage and motivate students to succeed.

Audience

Once again, the purpose will guide the next stage of the portfolio process, determining the audience. Showcase and growth portfolios are often intended for the student, teacher, classmates, and parents to view and discuss. In this light, portfolios need to be designed so outside onlookers will understand their intent. Mueller (2003a) also points out that the audience will shape a portfolio's construction, such as including a cover page or table of contents, to assist someone unfamiliar with navigating through the portfolio.

Oftentimes, knowing the audience motivates and encourages students to produce quality work. As an example, consider once more the writing process. In the authors' classrooms, audiences have included buddy groups, staff members, assembly participants, and publication sources such as school newsletters, the local newspaper, and writing contests. Audiences of this nature provide a powerful incentive and inspiration for students to perform to the best of their ability. Section V, *Sharing the Portfolio*, describes audiences and presentation settings in further detail.

Download a KWL chart from the ReadingQuest.org strategies web page at http://curry.edschool.virginia.edu/go/readquest/strat/kwl.html

The *Problem-Based Learning with Multimedia* web site focuses on media activities. However, the section, *Defining Your Audience*, offers useful guidelines for introducing and discussing an audience:
http://pblmm.k12.ca.us/PBLGuide/Activities/DefiningAudience.html

"As students become comfortable with the portfolio process, parents can become involved. This strengthens the motivation seen in students."

Cora Gaillard, Grade 5 Teacher

Criteria and Selection Process

It is important to bear in mind that at the beginning of introducing any new process, the focus is on the process itself. Therefore, it is worthwhile to begin small. As teachers and students become more familiar and proficient with the process, a greater variety and complexity of work samples, student choice, and reflection skills can be introduced. At the beginning, however, considerations of the process need to be simplistic in nature to avoid becoming overwhelmed. Such considerations include portfolio criteria and the work sample selection process.

Portfolio criteria. An important principle of authentic assessment is to inform students of the criteria for the assignment. At the onset of the portfolio project, teachers need to establish and share expectations and guidelines with the class. This enables learners to foster a vision of what entails a portfolio as a whole. Discussing specific criteria and showing exemplars of quality work motivates students to achieve high standards. Checklists are a popular method to instruct and guide student performance. Figure 2 provides an example of a portfolio checklist for the primary grades.

Figure 2. A portfolio checklist.

Name _____ Date _____

Type of Portfolio:_____

My Portfolio Checklist

1. My portfolio has a title page.

2. The first page in my portfolio is the Table of Contents.

3. I have included three entries of my best work.

4. A self-reflection sheet is attached to each entry.

5. Each piece of work includes the date.

6. My work is in the proper order.

As indicated in the example, checklists focus on specific instructional requirements and usually identify the presence or absence of a behavior (BC Primary Teachers' Association, 1992). Constructing checklists consists of using knowledge of child development and identifying the outcomes expected in a clear, concise, and specific manner (1992). Once students become proficient with the portfolio process, they will be able to follow a more encompassing set of criteria as well as providing input into the selection of criteria. Perhaps a goal for educators is to empower students in the upper intermediate grades with the capabilities of completing the three-step portfolio process as outlined by the *North Central Regional Educational Laboratory*. The first step in the process requires students to organize their work samples. Next, two reflections are to be completed based on a series of questions. The final component requests students to evaluate their growth and development and set goals for continuous progress.

Rubrics are another popular tool that outline the knowledge and skills that a "particular project or performance demonstrates, based on specific criteria for quality work" (Fiderer, 1999, p. 5). Marzano, Pickering, and Pollock (2001) point out that feedback specific to a criterion "tells students where they stand relative to a specific target of knowledge or skill" (p. 98). This premise is supported by research that "has consistently indicated that criterion-referenced feedback has a more powerful effect on student learning than norm-referenced feedback" (as cited in Marzano et al., 2001, pp. 98-99). Rubric assessments connect evaluation and learning by accomplishing the following (Fiderer, 1999, p. 11):

- focuses and streamlines curriculum planning;
- makes scoring of complex work products easier;
- establishes criteria for students' self-assessments;
- identifies steps students must take to improve a performance;
- shows growth in students' work over time;
- offers specific information to share with parents; and
- provides criteria for reporting on students.

As with checklists, teachers discuss the rubric at the beginning of the portfolio process so students are mindful of the criteria. Showing portfolio examples along with the rubric will ensure student understanding of what constitutes quality work as well as reinforce the criteria. "[W]hen students study

This three-step portfolio process can be accessed at http://www.ncrel.org/sdrs/areas/issues/methods/assment/as5selfe.htm

For more information on rubrics, visit Jon Mueller's *Authentic Assessment Toolbox* at http://jonathan.mueller.faculty.noctrl.edu/toolbox/rubrics.htm

Create your own rubrics at the following web sites:

Teachnology
http://www.teachnology.com/web_tools/rubrics/

RubiStar
http://rubistar.4teachers.org/index.php

and compare examples ranging in quality—from very strong to very weak—they are better able to internalize the differences" (McTighe & O'Connor, 2005, p. 14). This process enables "students to more accurately self-assess and improve their work before turning it in to the teacher" (p. 14). Table 1 presents a rubric using similar criteria as outlined in the checklist in figure 2.

Table 1
Sample of a Portfolio Rubric

PORTFOLIO RUBRIC				
	4 **Polished Work**	**3** **Just Needs a Little More Work**	**2** **Needs Some More Work**	**1** **Needs Much More Work**
Organization	My portfolio pages are in the proper order.	Most of the portfolio pages are in the proper order.	I need to put a few pages in the proper order.	I need to put most of my work in the proper order.
Title Page and Table of Contents	Title page is neat and colourful. The table of contents is nicely printed with no errors; items are listed in the correct order.	Title page is neat and colourful. The table of contents is nicely printed; items are listed in the correct order. I need to correct one or two minor errors.	I need to add more colour to the title page and list items in the proper order in the table of contents. I also need to correct some errors.	I need to make my title page neater and more colourful. I must also list items in the proper order in the table of contents. I need to proofread my work carefully to correct errors.
Entries	My portfolio has three entries of my best work with reflection sheets; all work is dated.	My portfolio has three entries of my best work with reflection sheets. I need to date one or two of the entries.	My portfolio has three entries of my best work. I need to complete one reflection sheet and add some dates to the entries.	Some entries are missing; I need to select more work samples from my collection and complete the reflection sheets.
Conventions	Very few spelling, grammar, or punctuation errors; mistakes do not distract from the content.	Some minor spelling, grammar, and/or punctuation errors to correct; mistakes do not distract from the content.	Some spelling, grammar, and/or punctuation errors that distract from the content. I need to proofread my work carefully to correct the mistakes.	Many errors that distract from the content; I need to proofread my work carefully to correct all of the spelling, grammar, and punctuation mistakes.

Selection process. The selection process begins with collecting work samples from which entries will be selected. Rolheiser et al. (2000) define work samples, also referred to as learning samples, and entries as follows:

> An important distinction between a portfolio learning sample and a portfolio entry is that a complete entry includes an element of reflection. Thus a portfolio entry is a learning sample *plus* a reflection on that sample. The reflection process transforms a collection of learning samples into a rich source of data because student reflection provides a more comprehensive and meaningful picture of individual learning. The collection of entries constitutes a portfolio. (p. 24)

Depending on the type of portfolio, teachers need to examine their programs to determine the products to collect. For example, a best work/celebration/showcase portfolio may consist of accumulating completed and polished classroom work in one or more curriculum areas. Growth portfolios, on the other hand, require items that reflect development and change over time. The list of possibilities is endless and may include items outlined in Figures 3 and 4.

Student Self-Reflection

Name: Quinn
Date: February 24th, 2006

Work Sample: Shape Picture on the open plains

I am proud of this entry that I chose for my portfolio because:
I am proud of the entry that I chose because I think I did a beautiful picture of shapes. It was a picture of two giraffes walking in the nice green grass on a sunny summer day in Africa.

Some new things that I learned are:
I learned about all sorts of different shapes and the ones I used in my picture are trapezoid, triangle, parallelogram and circle.

Signature: Quinn.

Grade 2 Work Sample

Figure 3. Best work portfolio items.

▪ Writing	✓ PowerPoint
▪ Research Reports	✓ database document
▪ Photos	✓ graphic designs
▪ Science Experiments	▪ Journal Entries
▪ Mathematical Computations and/or Problem Solving Activities	▪ Artwork
▪ Graphic Organizers	▪ Maps
✓ venn diagrams	▪ Achievement/Recognition Awards
✓ timelines	▪ Cassette and Video Tapes
✓ sequencing activities	✓ oral reading
✓ KWL charts	✓ athletic skills and sports
✓ Graphs	✓ plays and presentations
✓ Story Maps and/or Webs	▪ Assessments
▪ Computer-generated Application Products or Disks	✓ rubrics
✓ word processing document	✓ self-assessment checklists
✓ spreadsheets	✓ quizzes and tests
	✓ observation sheets

11

Figure 4. Growth portfolio items.

- rough drafts and final copies
- earlier work/later work
- writing process components (e.g., prewriting, drafting, editing, proofreading, publishing, and presenting)
- sample page from a reading text at different times of the year
- reading log or record of books read during a term or year
- KWL charts
- goal setting sheets
- assessments:
  - ✓ performance standards
  - ✓ rubrics
  - ✓ reading fluency probes and running records
  - ✓ pre and post quizzes and tests (e.g., spelling and basic facts)
  - ✓ curriculum based measurement
  - ✓ surveys
  - ✓ self-evaluation sheets

The portfolio process enables teachers to use existing curriculum activities without being faced with an additional workload. It then becomes a matter of organizing and managing the work products. The process of collecting samples from which entries will be selected is termed a *working portfolio*. A system for saving the working portfolio items may consist of large envelopes, file folders, or expandable folders. Teachers will then need to create a classroom storehouse system such as a file cabinet, shelves, bankers or file boxes, a chart box, or tubs and bins.

Once students begin selecting work samples for entries, they will require a presentation format for their portfolio. This is another opportunity for students to participate in the process by brainstorming various formats such as a binder, photo album, pizza box, scrapbook, or presentation board. There are many portfolio covers available for students to decorate their portfolios or they may prefer to design and create their own. Students will become motivated as they experience their portfolios taking shape.

Check out the abcteach web site for a variety of portfolio title pages and covers in all subject areas as well as for specific grades:

http://www.abcteach.com/directory/portfolios/portfolio_covers/special_interests/

http://www.abcteach.com/directory/portfolios/portfolio_covers/grade_level_covers/

The next phase of the selection process is determining who will select the entries. Portfolios present an opportune time for students to become engaged in the assessment process. By being involved in the selection of entries, students take an active and accurate role in telling the story of their learning. It is the students' insight into what constitutes quality or best work that will enable them to analyze achievement and monitor their learning progress. The teacher's role is best served as a facilitator to guide student choices. This encompasses the following:

- promoting a collaborative and comfortable learning environment;
- creating a portfolio along with the class and modeling the selection process;
- asking questions to promote and direct thinking, understanding, and decision making;
- incorporating peer and parent involvement and collaboration in the selection process to provide students with suggestions and/or feedback; and
- emphasizing student ownership and responsibility for their learning achievement and accomplishments.

Time Frame

The decision-making process continues with considering the time frame for the selection process. For teachers just beginning the portfolio process, "a short-term experience can build early success for the teacher and can help build confidence for future refinement and expansion" (Rolheiser et al., 2000, pp. 6-7). Short-term selections may consist of choosing entries every two weeks or on a monthly basis. Time periods will be influenced by decisions related to the purpose, type of portfolio, audience, and the contents. For instance, in reference to the examples of using writing pieces with performance standards and reading fluency probes and running records, three terms per year is an appropriate period of time for students to experience and reflect on growth. Samples that are not selected during a particular time period may be taken home and the next round of collecting work begins.

Davies (2000b) provides helpful information when considering the time frame:

Student Self-Reflection

Name: Dane
Date: October 24, 2005

Work Sample: Math Test

I am proud of this entry that I chose for my portfolio because:

I chose my math test because I got 100 percent on it. It was fun. I didn't cheat. I tried my best. I concentrated on it.

Some new things that I learned are:

I didn't know the crocodile math. I learned less than and greater than but I had trouble a little bit.

Signature: Dane

Student Self-Reflection

Name: Katelyn
Date: Oct. 24, 2005

Work Sample: The Rainforest

This piece of work makes me feel a little bit mad **because...** I wish I could do it over. I didn't do good on it. I am still mad about it.

Something that I still need to work on is:

I need to read carefully for meaning.

Signature: Katelyn

Grade 2 Work Samples

If you've decided to show growth or progress and are using a progress portfolio as part of the reporting process, then you will probably want to do some initial entries and some entries at each reporting period—a total of three or four entries per year. If you've selected to do a best work or process portfolio, then you may decide to select entries weekly, monthly, or term by term. (¶ 9)

Table 2 provides a summary of the portfolio elements discussed so far for teachers to consider when planning.

PARENT/GUARDIAN RESPONSE SHEET FOR PORTFOLIO REVIEW

Two Stars:

Marissa, your portfolio was great! You have very nice printing and the art was amazing!

Turkey math was very cool. You are very good at math.

One Wish:

Marissa, I would like you to listen more carefully to what you are reading so you know what you have read and remember it.

Thank You

Parent of a Grade 2 Student

Table 2
Planning Outline Summary

PORTFOLIO CONTENTS	
Best Work/Celebration/Showcase Portfolio	**Growth Portfolio**
• Decide which curriculum area(s) to focus on (e.g., writing, reading, mathematics, art) • Determine and collect samples of work from which entries will be selected	• Decide which curriculum area(s) to focus on (e.g., writing, reading, mathematics, art) • Determine and collect student samples over time from which entries will be selected

PORTFOLIO CRITERIA

• **Provide students with the criteria for the portfolio:**
  ✓ title/cover page
  ✓ amount/type of entries
  ✓ table of contents
  ✓ self-reflection sheets
  ✓ dates on all items
  ✓ letter to viewers/letter of introduction/cover letter/"all about me" activities
  ✓ portfolio criteria format (e.g., rubric, checklist, self-evaluation)

ORGANIZATION/MANAGEMENT	

• **Choose a working portfolio and student presentation method:**
  ✓ file/pocket folder
  ✓ three tang report cover/binder
  ✓ accordion/expandable file folder
  ✓ large envelope
  ✓ photo album
  ✓ scrapbook
  ✓ pizza or cereal box
  ✓ presentation board
	• **Select a classroom storage system:**
	  ✓ shelves
	  ✓ bankers/file boxes
	  ✓ file cabinet
	  ✓ chart box
	  ✓ tubs/bins/trays

SELECTION PROCESS	

• **Selection of entries by:**
  ✓ student
  ✓ teacher
  ✓ student and teacher
  ✓ parent
  ✓ student and parent
  ✓ student and peer(s)/buddies
	• **Review collection of work samples to select entries:**
	  ✓ weekly
	  ✓ upon completion of an activity/unit
	  ✓ every two weeks
	  ✓ monthly
	  ✓ once per term

Self-reflection

It is during the reflection stage that students practice self-evaluation to promote learning. Stiggins (2001) captures the essence of the role of self-reflection in the portfolio process: "Of all the dimensions of portfolios, the process of self-reflection is the most important.... One way to hold them [students] accountable for achieving a clear sense of themselves as learners is to have them write or talk about that accumulating evidence" (p. 478).

Decisions regarding self-reflection activities need to relate to the purpose. As stated previously, the purpose may be to highlight and celebrate best work or growth. In this case, the following examples of questions and prompts will guide children to reflect on their learning:

- "What makes this your best piece?" (Andersen, n.d., p. 2)
- "Why did you select this piece of work?" (p. 2)
- What makes your best work different from other or least best work? (Andersen, n.d.)
- "What do you know about _____ (e.g., the scientific method) that you did not know at the beginning of the year (or term, etc.)?" (Mueller, 2003a, p. 12)
- "One skill I could not perform very well but now I can is...." (p. 12)
- "How has your _____ (e.g., writing) changed since last year?" (p. 12)
- "Looking at (or thinking about) an earlier piece of similar work, how does this new piece of work compare? How is it better or worse? Where can you see progress or improvement?" (p. 12)

Such prompts can be used to create self-reflection sheets that students attach to items displayed in the portfolio (see Figure 5). Younger students can reflect on their performances without writing (Niguidula, 2005). Students in higher grades can scribe for primary children using prompts prepared by the teacher. Using video or audiotape of students responding to self-reflection questions is an effective way of meeting needs of beginning writers. See more examples of prompts for classroom use in Appendix A.

Check out the following web site for useful tips on self-reflection:
http://www.qesnrecit.qc.ca/portfolio/eng/theory-R.htm

For more self-reflection forms, access the following page at the abcteach web site:
http://www.abcteach.com/directory/portfolios/goalsevaluations/

Figure 5. Self-reflection form sample.

SELF-REFLECTION

Name:_____ Date:_____

Work Sample: _____

I am selecting this entry for my portfolio because:

_____

_____

_____

Some things that I did to make this product my best work are:

_____

_____

_____

Signature_____

Goal Setting. Self-reflection presents an opportunity to introduce goal setting. "Broadly defined, goal setting is the process of establishing a direction for learning. It is a skill that successful people have mastered to help them realize both short-term and long-term desires" (Marzano et al., 2001, p. 93). Essentially, students identify areas for improvement to set goals that will enhance their progress over time and ultimately guide them towards becoming more responsible for their learning. Following are some examples of goal setting questions and prompts:

- What is one thing that you can improve upon in this piece? (Mueller, 2003a)
- "What is one way that you will try to improve your _____ (e.g., writing)?" (p. 13)

"Portfolios encourage self-reflection and teach children to learn to be proud of themselves and their accomplishments. In addition to this, they allow students to find areas for self-improvement."

Nicole Person, Grade 2 Teacher

- What is a realistic goal for the end of the term? (2003a)
- "I will work toward my goal by…." (p. 13)
- "If you could work further on this piece, what would you do?" (Andersen, n.d., p. 2)
- "I could do further work on this project by…." (BC Primary Teacher's Association, 1992, p. 7.11)
- "What I would do differently another time is…." (p. 7.11)
- One thing that I still need to work on is….

The BC Primary Teachers' Association (1992) provides some useful suggestions and guidelines to consider when introducing the self-evaluation process:

- Mutual respect and trust must exist between you and the students. You must be honest with students, yet demonstrate your belief that they can make responsible decisions and assess their own growth. You must be accepting and non-judgmental.
- The first few times students are self-evaluating, have them focus on just one or two aspects.
- Frequently hold individual teacher-student conferences to discuss self-evaluation.
- Hold class discussions to clarify important goals and select criteria for self-evaluation. (p. 7.6)

Planning

"Portfolios illustrate students' efforts, progress and achievements in an organized and structured way" (Meisels, 1997, p. 7).

By planning and deciding on the key elements of the portfolio process discussed in this section, teachers and students will enjoy and experience the many benefits of portfolio assessment. Figure 6 outlines a planning form to assist teachers in the decision-making process.

GOAL SETTING

Name: McKenzie
Date: Jan. 20

Work Sample:
Write Before School

What I noticed:
I was only writing 3 to 4 lines at the beginning of the year. After a while I started writing 5-7 lines. Now I write 2 whole pages!

My goal: is to write 2-3 pages!

Grade 4 Work Sample

For a synopsis of a teacher's grade four class on the use of portfolios and other authentic assessment methods at the beginning, middle, and end of the school year, read *Authentic Classroom Assessment in Action.* Ms. Rodriguez's Classroom at http://www.eduplace.com/rdg/res/lit ass/class.html.

Figure 6. Teacher planning form.

TEACHER PORTFOLIO PLANNING FORM

Purpose/Type of Portfolio:

☐ Best Work/Celebration/Showcase ☐ Highlight Growth

Other_____

Curriculum Area(s)/Content:

☐ Reading ☐ Writing ☐ Mathematics ☐ Science

☐ Social Studies Other: _____

Content(s)/Item(s): _____

Audience:

☐ Teacher(s) ☐ Parents/Family ☐ Peers ☐ Buddy Class

Other: _____

Time Frame:

☐ Every Two Weeks ☐ Monthly ☐ Beginning/End of Year

☐ Each Term Other:_____

Self-Reflection Question(s)/Prompt(s): (record on back of page)

Portfolio Criteria Format:

☐ Checklist ☐ Rubric ☐ Conference

Other: _____

Section III: Instructional Strategies and Applications

Current research contributes to many literature sources that describe effective instructional strategies to increase student learning and achievement. Along with successful classroom practices and research on how the brain learns, teachers can implement quality instruction to optimize student success of the portfolio process. These strategies include activating prior knowledge, establishing criteria for tasks, modeling, providing descriptive feedback, and using cooperative learning and peer evaluation. The following pages describe each instructional method based on literature as well as practical suggestions and applications to guide lesson planning.

Activating Prior Knowledge

Literature sources state:

"Tasks designed to assess and activate students' prior knowledge can serve many purposes" (Crandall, Jaramillo, Olsen, & Peyton, 2001, p. 50):
- shows "teachers immediately what their students know or don't know about a topic" (p. 50)
- provides "immediate links to the theme or topic by showing students that what they're studying connects directly to their own lives, thus establishing personal relevance and interest" (p. 50)
- "By relating new information to knowledge already stored in their long-term memories, people find *meaning* in that information" (University of Phoenix, 2002, p. 270).
- "Meaningful learning appears to facilitate both storage and retrieval: The information goes in more quickly and is remembered more easily" (as cited in University of Phoenix, 2002, p. 270).
- Students "can profit from the use of not just one, but several, activities that allow them to uncover what they already know about a topic and see how it relates to their own lives, before they begin to study the lesson content" (Crandall et al., 2001, p. 50).

Applications:

Introduction to the Portfolio Process:
- When introducing the portfolio process, ask students to bring a photo album from home. Lead a discussion as to its purpose and contents:
  - ✓ What is a photo album used for? (to store/collect pictures; capture special moments and milestones; record stages of childhood and/or adulthood)
  - ✓ Name some times when we usually take pictures. (birthdays, holidays, special events/occasions, visits from relatives and friends, sports)

Activating Prior Knowledge continued...

- ✓ Is there any written information to describe the pictures? If so, what information is recorded? (names, dates, places, occasions)
- ✓ Find two or three pictures that are your favourites. Why are these your favourites? (answers will vary)
- ✓ Are there any times that you would have liked pictures taken to include in the album? Are there any photos that you do not like? Why? (answers will vary)
- ✓ How can your photo album be improved? (answers will vary)
- ✓ What does the photo album say about your family? (answers will vary)

Have students follow this discussion outline to share their photo albums with a partner or small group (use Appendix B as a handout or overhead). Tie together the relationship and similarities between photo albums and portfolios (e.g., collecting items for a purpose).

- Teachers can also use this activity to compare a photo album with a portfolio. After students examine the photo albums, use portfolio examples to lead a discussion about its purpose and contents. Students will then have information to compare the album to a portfolio. Venn diagrams can be used to list the differences and similarities. Download a Venn diagram along with teaching and instructional guidelines at <http://curry.edschool.virginia.edu/go/readquest/strat/venn.html>.
  Teachers who are new to the portfolio process and have not yet had the opportunity to collect examples can use images from electronic portfolio sites. The *Tammy Worcester* web site posts two portfolio examples that include title pages, introductory letters, and entries: <http://www.essdack.org/port/index.html>.

- Another way to introduce portfolios is to brainstorm some methods of capturing, collecting, and displaying memories of everyday life and special occasions. Responses may include the following:

  - ✓ framed pictures and certificates/awards
  - ✓ photo albums
  - ✓ journals
  - ✓ videos
  - ✓ digital pictures
  - ✓ letters and cards from friends and relatives

  Teachers can then relate these ideas to the purpose of the portfolio process (e.g., collecting and presenting work to illustrate best work or growth). Students can also look up the definition of portfolio in the dictionary or computer to connect the two concepts (i.e., methods of collecting memories and portfolios). The following web page provides a portfolio definition and description that is appropriate for the intermediate grades: <http://www.funderstanding.com/portfolio_assessment.cfm>.
  The *Problem-Based Learning with Multimedia* web site outlines steps for a general brainstorming session: <http://pblmm.k12.ca.us/PBLGuide/Activities/brainstorm.html>.

- KWL charts provide an opportunity for students to access background knowledge by describing what they already know about a topic (e.g., portfolios). The *ReadingQuest* web site stated earlier provides guidelines to presenting a KWL chart as well two samples to download.

Establish and Introduce Criteria

Literature sources state:

- Criteria is defined as "'guidelines, rules, characteristics, or dimensions that are used to judge the quality of student performance. Criteria indicate what we value in student responses, products, or performances'" (as cited in "Performance Critieria," n.d., ¶ 1).
- "Good-quality criteria provide clear instructional targets for teachers and learning targets for students"(Arter & McTighe, 2001, p. xi).
- "If we want students to take control of their own learning, they must know the criteria for quality" (p. xii). "When students know the criteria in advance of their performance, they have clear goals for their work…. [S]tudents don't need to guess what is most important or how teachers will judge their work" (McTighe & O'Connor, 2005, p. 13).
- "Involving students in generating and using criteria for self- and peer assessment helps them 'get their minds around' important elements of quality and use that knowledge to improve their own performance" (p. xi).
- To create criteria for a good performance on a task, teachers need to ask themselves "'what does good performance on this task look like?'" (Mueller, 2003b, ¶ 1).
- A good criterion consists of the following characteristics (Characteristics of a Good Criterion section, ¶ 1):

  ✓ a clearly stated;
  ✓ brief;
  ✓ observable;
  ✓ statement of behaviour; and
  ✓ written in language students understand.

- Mueller also provides the following questions for teachers and students to consider when developing criteria:

  Teacher: "Do [the criteria] make sense to you? Can you distinguish one from another? Can you envision examples of each? Are they all worth assessing?" (How Many Criteria do you Need for a Task? section, ¶ 2):

  Students: "Do [the criteria] make sense to them? Do they understand their relationship to the task? Do they know how they would use the criteria to begin their work? To check their work?" (¶ 3)

For more information, visit Jon Mueller's web page, *Identify the Criteria for the Task,* at <http://jonathan.mueller.faculty.noctrl.edu/toolbox/howstep3.htm>.

Applications:

Introduction to Selecting Entries and Self-reflection:
1. Introduce the term "self-reflection" by referring to the photo album activity. Review the discussion points regarding analyzing the album by choosing favourite pictures and giving suggestions for improving the collection. Tie together this process to self-reflection in which students analyze their work.

Criteria continued...

2. Teachers can also use vocabulary graphic organizers in which students engage in activities to enhance the understanding of new words. Check out the word definition activities at the following web sites:
   edHelper: <http://www.edhelperclipart.com/clipart/teachers/org-wordweb.pdf >.
   More graphic organizers at edHelper:
   <http://www.edhelper.com/teachers/graphic_organizers.htm>.
   ReadQuest.org: <http://curry.edschool.virginia.edu/go/readquest/strat/wordmap.html>.

3. Next, brainstorm a list of criteria that students believe they need in order to produce quality work. Brainstorming responses may include the following:
   - ✓ focusing during instruction and following directions
   - ✓ thinking carefully about ideas
   - ✓ being creative and original
   - ✓ taking risks and "thinking outside the box"
   - ✓ demonstrating an understanding of ideas and concepts
   - ✓ following criteria for assignment
   - ✓ gathering and using necessary resources (e.g., dictionary, thesaurus)
   - ✓ asking for help when needed and applying suggestions from the teacher or peers
   - ✓ printing/writing neatly
   - ✓ checking/proofreading work for spelling, punctuation, and grammatical errors

4. The number and quality of responses will vary depending on the grade level. A tendency of students, particularly in the primary grades, is to use words such as "good," "nice," and "cool" (e.g., "I picked this work sample because it is nice."). Guide students to more specific statements by asking questions such as:
   - ✓ What makes your work good?
   - ✓ What did you do to produce good work?
   - ✓ Why is your work nice? /What makes your work nice?

5. Next, discuss personal feelings, reactions, and thoughts that students may experience from producing quality work:
   - ✓ feeling proud or pleased
   - ✓ a sense of personal satisfaction, accomplishment, or success
   - ✓ enjoyment from acquiring knowledge, skills, and/or attitudes
   - ✓ sense of motivation to continue to achieve and succeed
   - ✓ recognizing and acknowledging the results of effort and perseverance
   - ✓ meaningful or significant connections to real life situations

6. Appendix C provides a format to list brainstorming responses. Post the list of criteria in the classroom and add to it throughout the year as students become more experienced with selecting entries and participating in self-reflection.

7. As mentioned earlier, checklists and rubrics are valuable methods to communicate criteria. The selected criteria should relate to the self-reflection prompt. Figure 7 presents a prompt, followed by a corresponding checklist. Table 3 uses similar criteria in the form of a rubric.

Figure 7. Reflection prompt and checklist.

SELF-REFLECTION

Name:_____ Date:_____

Work Sample:_____

I am selecting this entry for my portfolio because:

_____

_____

_____

_____

What I would do differently another time is:

_____

_____

_____

_____

Signature:_____

Name:_____ Date:_____

Entry:_____

My Self-Reflection Checklist

1. I explained why I chose this entry for my portfolio. ☐

2. I gave a useful suggestion for something that I would do another time. ☐

3. My work is printed neatly. ☐

4. Sentences are complete. ☐

5. Spelling, punctuation, and grammar are corrected. ☐

6. My self-reflection includes the date. ☐

7. The self-reflection sheet is attached to my entry. ☐

Table 3
Rubric for Self-reflection

	4 Polished Work	3 Just Needs a Little More Work	2 Needs Some More Work	1 Needs Much More Work
SELF-REFLECTION RUBRIC				
Self-Reflection	Clearly, specifically describes the reason for selecting the entry; a useful suggestion is given for another time.	Clearly describes the reason for selecting the entry; a useful suggestion is given for another time.	I need to describe my reason for selecting the entry more clearly; a suggestion is given for another time.	The reflection is not clear and needs more detail.
Word Choice	Words are specific and accurately describe what I want to tell; readers would know something about me as a learner.	Most words are specific and describe what I want to tell; readers would know something about me as a learner.	Some words need to be more specific to accurately describe what I want to tell and so readers would know more about me as a learner.	I used simple words such as "good" and "nice." I need to use specific words and more detail so readers will know something about me as a learner.
Mechanics	Sentences are complete; very few spelling, grammar, or punctuation errors; mistakes do not distract from the content.	Sentences are complete; some minor spelling, grammar, and/or punctuation errors to correct; mistakes do not distract from the content.	Some sentences are run-ons or incomplete; spelling, grammar, and/or punctuation errors distract from the content. I need to proofread my work carefully to correct the mistakes.	My sentences are incomplete and difficult to understand; many errors distract from the content. I need to proofread my work carefully to correct all of the spelling, grammar, and punctuation mistakes.
Neatness	Work is neatly written/printed and includes the date; the self-reflection sheet is attached to the entry.	Work is neatly printed/written with one or two distracting errors (e.g., letters or words written over). The self-reflection sheet is dated and attached to the entry.	Some of the work is difficult to read. I need to check it for messiness and letters or words that are written over. I need to make sure that the self-reflection sheet is dated and attached to the entry.	Many of the words are hard to read. My work needs to be neater so it is easier to read. I also need to add the date and attach the self-reflection sheet to the entry.

Modeling and Self-Reflection

Literature Sources State:

- Effective programs integrate modeling as a method to foster skill development. "When modeling is accompanied by thinking aloud, students can hear the teacher/writer sort through various options and questions and make choices appropriate for the intended purpose and audience" (Hampton, 1995, p. 107).
- This approach provides students with "specific, concrete examples of how to process information effectively" (University of Phoenix, 2002, p. 380). Additionally, such practices "help students become aware of their own thinking strategies" (Kline, 1995, p. 30).
- Modeling is also effective when teachers adhere to the old adage, practice what you preach. "When modeling, teachers in whatever subject area follow the same assignments or suggestions that they give their students" (Kline, 1995, p. 31).

Applications:

1. By creating a portfolio along with the class, teachers can model various elements of the process. Contents for a teacher portfolio may include the following:
   - ✓ lesson plans, units, and instructional methods
   - ✓ practices to improve teaching such as attending workshops and reading current literature on effective instructional strategies
   - ✓ description of workshops and presentations to students, staff, and parents
   - ✓ statement of educational philosophy
   - ✓ testimonials of teaching attributes from administrators, staff, parents, and students
   - ✓ leadership skills
   - ✓ committees, extra-curricular activities, field trips
   - ✓ student assessment and evaluation methods
   - ✓ course work products
   - ✓ teaching awards and recognition
2. Teachers can model the self-reflection activity while thinking aloud: "I am selecting this entry for my teaching portfolio because…."
3. Allow students to provide feedback to the teacher's self-reflection process by using established criteria:
   - ✓ Does the self-reflection clearly describe the reason for selecting the entry?
   - ✓ Are the words specific and tell something about me as a learner?
   - ✓ Are the sentences complete?
   - ✓ Are there any spelling, punctuation, or grammatical errors?
   - ✓ Is the date included?
4. Follow the teacher's modeling session with anonymous student self-reflections. Use examples from previous years or another class. If samples are not available, teachers can create some hypothetical reflections. Begin with a good example to reinforce the criteria. Follow with a mediocre self-reflection, then a weak illustration so students can practice identifying criteria that are missing and suggestions for improvement.

Provide Descriptive Feedback

Literature Sources State:
- Research reveals that "the most powerful single modification that enhances achievement is feedback. The simplest prescription for improving education must be 'dollops of feedback'" (as cited in Marzano, 2001, p. 96).
- "Descriptive feedback tells students about their learning—what is working (do more of this) and what is not (do less of this)" (Davies, 2000a, p. 12).
- "Wiggins defined feedback fairly simply: 'Feedback tells you what you just did. Feedback is information you can use. It's descriptive and useful information about what you did and didn't do in light of a goal'" (Wilcox, 2006, p. 6).
- "The most effective feedback identifies success and also offers students a recipe for corrective action" (as cited in Chappuis, 2005, p. 41).
- "To be effective, feedback needs to cause thinking…that addresses what the student needs to do to improve, linked to rubrics where appropriate" (Leahy et al., 2005, p. 22).
- "Involving students in assessment and increasing the amount of descriptive feedback while decreasing evaluative feedback increases student learning significantly. While all students show significant gains, students who usually achieve the least show the largest gains overall" (as cited in Davies, 2000a, p. 9).
- "Some [parents] even said they found comments more useful than grades because the comments provided them with guidance on how to help their children" (Leahy et al., 2005, p. 23).

Applications:
- Using rubrics, instruct students to highlight in yellow the criteria that they feel represents the quality of their work (as cited in Chappuis, 2005). "On the same scoring guide [rubrics], highlight in blue the phrases that you think describe their work" (p. 42). Green sections indicate a match between the student and teacher's assessment whereas criteria that remain blue or yellow show a discrepancy (2005). Teachers then use this guide to focus on areas for descriptive feedback, either in the form of a conference or written comments.
- Conduct short conferences with students (e.g., 5 to 10 minutes) using rubrics or checklists as a basis for discussing students' strengths, needs, and future goals.
- Feedback from teachers in the form of comments provides students with information that highlight their abilities as well as areas requiring improvement and possible goals. As illustrated in Appendix D, comment sections can be added to rubrics.
- Parents play an important role in contributing valuable descriptive feedback. Provide parents with the opportunity to review and respond to their child's work in the same manner described here for teachers. In addition, prepare forms specifically designed for parental feedback as illustrated in Figure 8.
- Additions to student self-reflection forms can include comment/feedback sections for different reviewers such as teachers, parents, and peers.
- Rubric categories serve as a guideline for establishing response sections that can be copied onto to the reverse side of the rubric (see Figure 9).

Figure 8. Parent response form.

PARENT/GUARDIAN RESPONSE SHEET:
PORTFOLIO REVIEW

☆ ☆ ☆ ☆ ☆ ☆ ☆ ☆ ☆

Dear Reviewer:

Research reveals that effective feedback identifies a learner's strengths as well as indicating areas requiring improvement. Please review your child's portfolio entries of best work. Fill in the *Two Stars* section with two positive comments about your child's progress and accomplishments. Suggest one wish that describes what you would like your child to focus on to improve his/her work.

Two Stars:

☆ _____

_____

_____

☆ _____

_____

_____

One Wish:

☆ _____

_____

_____

_____

Signature of Reviewer: _____   Date: _____

Source: Adapted from Nicole Person's teacher created material. Used with permission.

Figure 9. Response sections to include with rubric.

SELF-REFLECTION RUBRIC				
	4 **Polished Work**	**3** **Just Needs a Little More Work**	**2** **Needs Some More Work**	**1** **Needs Much More Work**
Self-Reflection	Teacher Feedback:			
	Parent Feedback:			
	Peer Feedback:			
Word Choice	Teacher Feedback:			
	Parent Feedback:			
	Peer Feedback:			
Mechanics	Teacher Feedback:			
	Parent Feedback:			
	Peer Feedback:			

Cooperative Learning and Peer Evaluation

Literature Sources State:

- Cooperative learning consists of students working in small groups to achieve a common goal (University of Phoenix, 2002).
- "Cooperative learning offers one means of having students learn from and help each other" (as cited in Crandall, Jaramillo, Olsen, & Peyton, 2001, p. 48).
- "As they [students] assess the work of a peer, they are forced to engage in understanding of the rubric, but in the context of someone else's work, which is less emotionally charged" (Leahy et al., 2005, p. 22).
- The BC Primary Teachers' Association (1992) outlines the following benefits of peer evaluation:
  - ✓ Peer appraisal identifies feelings and attitudes among students that you may have been unable to detect through direct observation.
  - ✓ Peer evaluation gives the students feedback beyond that provided by you. This feedback helps the students confirm, clarify, and extend their own ideas and feelings. It also helps them be more aware of their role as a class member or a small group member.
  - ✓ Peer evaluation helps the students more clearly see their role in the group. They learn to look at an issue from different points of view, to listen carefully, and to respect the opinions of others. They learn to seek consensus and how to formulate sound conclusions. (p. 7.20)

Applications:

- Provide opportunities for students to share individual entries and whole portfolios with peers. As mentioned previously, teachers can model the process by creating a teaching portfolio. This then allows them to model the peer evaluation process using established criteria and the class as respondents.
- Have students begin the evaluation by focusing on one or two positive features of their peer's entry or portfolio (BC Primary Teachers' Association, 1992). For example, peers can make two comments on what they liked or found interesting about the work. Many of the self-reflection prompts are also appropriate to guide peer evaluation (e.g., "My favourite part is…" or "Some strengths of your work are…"). A section for student comments can also be added to the self-reflection activities (see Appendix E).
- When students become more proficient with commenting and responding to each other's work, suggestions for improvement can become part of the peer evaluation (e.g., "A suggestion for improvement is…" or "More detail is needed to…").
- Helpful teaching tips and guidelines for student-led discussions can be accessed at <http://pblmm.k12.ca.us/PBLGuide/Activities/studentdiscussions.html>.
- Appendix F provides a classroom poster of guidelines for partner or small group sessions.

Section IV: Expanding the Portfolio Process

As mentioned earlier, it is best to begin the teaching and learning of any new process in a simplistic manner. Once teachers and students have experience with the portfolio process itself, more comprehensive elements can be introduced. Integrating prescribed learning outcomes or standards into the process opens the door to increased opportunities and possibilities of expanding portfolio use. Additionally, "when a student has to defend why an entry in his or her portfolio fulfills a particular learning expectation, the student will more thoroughly understand that expectation" (Niguidula, 2005, p. 47). At the same time, language and organizational components that align with existing graduation programs can become part of the framework. This section uses the BC prescribed learning outcomes and graduation portfolio program to illustrate how to transform the portfolio process in this way.

Curriculum and the Portfolio Process

Prescribed curriculum, established by districts and provinces or states, sets the stage for building a more extensive portfolio. Learning outcomes or standards in themselves provide the basis for identifying portfolio content. "Learning outcomes set out the knowledge, enduring ideas, issues, concepts, skills, and attitudes for each subject" (BC Ministry of Education, 1996a, p. III). By selecting an outcome in a core subject, such as language arts, teachers can use the specific statements to list criteria for portfolios. Consider the following language arts prescribed learning outcome for *Grade 5 – Comprehend and Respond (Comprehension)*: "It is expected that students will demonstrate their understanding of written, oral, and visual communications" (BC Ministry of Education, 1996a, p. 80). Within this learning outcome are more qualifying statements that present the objective in a precise, teachable format. These consist of the following (p. 80):

PARENT/GUARDIAN RESPONSE SHEET FOR PORTFOLIO REVIEW

Two Stars:
Very interesting writing style.

Wonderful art work. Also enjoyed listening to the tape.

One Wish:
I can never see enough of Serena's creative mind, so more would be better.

Thank You

Parent of a Grade 5 Student

It is *expected that students will:*

- demonstrate understanding of the main ideas or events in print (including stories and poetry) and in non-print media
- extend their understanding of a given selection by developing related questions and activities
- use a variety of written and graphic forms, including charts, webs, and maps, to organize details and information
- locate and interpret details to answer specific questions or to complete tasks
- describe information contained in simple and direct illustrations, maps, charts, or other graphic representations.

Using such prescribed learning outcomes and standards as a basis to develop criteria for portfolios presents increased opportunities for teaching and learning. Portfolio assessment is non-linear in nature. This implies that there are many different paths in which teachers and students can follow. Consider the following opportunities and benefits:

Student choice and decision-making. Students can choose a predetermined number of learning outcomes and provide the corresponding evidence from classroom assignments and activities. Choice is an important component of graduation portfolios, which can constitute a large percentage of the overall mark. In reference to the *Graduation Portfolio Program* in BC, "students choose areas in which they want to submit Portfolio Choice evidence for up to 50% of the Graduation Portfolio mark" (BC Ministry of Education, 2004, p. 3). By integrating choice and decision making into the portfolio process, students experience ownership and responsibility for their learning.

Metacognition. Students can focus on strategies that best suit their learning style. In choosing from the list of reading outcomes, some students comprehend text best from using a chart to organize information, while others may prefer to develop questions to further their understanding of material.

Flexibility for teachers. Educators have much flexibility to include outcomes that they deem important as part of the portfolio criteria. Using the list of reading outcomes, for example, teachers may consider the first outcome a priority

---

STUDENT RESPONSE SHEET FOR PORTFOLIO REVIEW

☆☆☆☆☆

Name: Daniel
Date: Oct. 25, 2005

Two Stars -- What I do well.
I work hard in class.

I listen at school.

One Wish -- What I can improve.
I can work hard at reading.

**Action Plan –
What I can do to improve.**
I can use my reading strategies.

I can read at home.

STUDENT RESPONSE SHEET FOR PORTFOLIO REVIEW

☆☆☆☆☆

Name: Marissa
Date: Oct. 25, 2005

Two Stars -- What I do well.
I do very good art. I have very pretty work.

I have very neat printing.

One Wish -- What I can improve.
I want to listen for the teacher's instructions more carefully.

**Action Plan –
What I can do to improve.**
I can start making eye contact with the teacher.

Grade 2 Work Samples

and, thus, include it as part of the expectations. Student choice may consist of one other learning outcome, thereby sharing the selection of criteria.

Promotes integration across the curriculum. By using learning outcomes, students can provide evidence from a variety of content areas. As an example, the grade five comprehend and respond outcomes apply to science and social studies activities as well as language arts. This enables students to use strategies in multiple contexts, thereby reinforcing techniques and promoting the transfer of knowledge—"to use what they know in a new situation" (McTighe & O'Conner, 2005, p. 12).

Streamlines teacher planning. Collecting evidence of learning for portfolios assists teachers in planning and implementing methods and activities to deliver curriculum requirements. Essentially, "teachers must give plenty of assignments that tap into the skills and knowledge represented by each standard" (Niguidula, 2005, p. 46). For example, in meeting the objective of using a variety of written and graphic forms to organize details and information, many types of graphic organizers are available for teachers to ensure that this particular learning outcome is achieved.

Meeting diverse needs of students. By varying the reading level of material to accommodate individuals, groups, or classes, all students can follow the criteria for the portfolio. Consider the outcome requiring students to locate and interpret details to answer specific questions or to complete tasks. The outcome remains constant while students with learning difficulties can be given text at their reading level. In contrast, students who would benefit from a challenge or enrichment can use material above grade level to meet their learning needs. In addition, expectations in terms of the number of criteria and the amount of time required to complete portfolio requirements can be adapted to meet individual student learning needs. Providing Aboriginal students and second-language learners with reading material that interests them and activities to celebrate and share their language, culture and heritage will optimize their learning experiences.

Incorporating activities from home and the community. "Portfolio evidence can be based on experiences and learning

---

GOAL SETTING

Name: Jordan
Date: Jan. 20, 2006

Work Sample:
Flat Stanley Letter

What I noticed: I noticed that I used sentences and paragraphs, but my verbs were not powerful and it wasn't very exciting.

My goal: My goal is to use more powerful verbs next time.

Grade 4 Work Sample

PARENT/GUARDIAN RESPONSE SHEET FOR PORTFOLIO REVIEW

Two Stars:
We love your poems and stories.

We love how you enjoy everything that you do and try to tackle things with such enthusiasm.

One Wish:
We wish that you would practice your mad minutes more at home with us.

Thank You

Parent of a Grade 2 Student

either in school courses, or through extra-curricular, home, or community activities" (BC Ministry of Education, 2004, p. 7). Accepting portfolio evidence in this manner promotes the partnership between the school and other stakeholders in the education system. In regards to the Personal Health aspect of the BC *Graduation Portfolio Program*, students must "engage in 80 hours, or more, of moderate or intense physical activity" (p. 77). This can consist of teams or clubs, individual sports, or recreation activities sponsored by the community or home.

Increases portfolio skills. Subjecting students to the language and format of curriculum and its connection to everyday learning builds knowledge and skills necessary to commence on a self-directed journey such as graduation portfolio programs.

Accountability. Providing collections of evidence to show that students are working towards or meeting specific learning outcomes represents accountability at its best.

Portfolio Language and Framework

In selecting portfolio language, teachers can align vocabulary at the elementary, middle, and junior secondary school levels with that of graduation programs. Key words and phrases that remain consistent throughout the elementary grades will ensure a smooth and successful transition to a senior secondary level portfolio process.

The BC *Graduation Portfolio Program* uses the term "organizer" to refer to subject areas or categories (e.g., Arts and Design, Information and Technology, Personal Health, etc.). Organizers at the elementary level, therefore, would consist of curriculum subject areas such as language arts, mathematics, social studies, science, fine arts, and physical education. In keeping with the graduation program format, portfolios that include more than one organizer would be numbered as follows:

1. Language Arts
2. Mathematics
3. Fine Arts

STUDENT RESPONSE SHEET FOR PORTFOLIO REVIEW

☆☆☆☆☆

Name: Dale
Date: Oct. 25, 2005

Two Stars -- What I do well.
I am friendly and kind to other people.

I know lots of sight words.

One Wish -- What I can improve.
I can work on staying on task.

Action Plan –
What I can do to improve.
I can ignore distractions.

Grade 2 Work Sample

Components of the organizers are referred to as "aspects." These are "statements of a skill or competency that the student must demonstrate" (BC Ministry of Education, 2005, p. 10). In using the prescribed learning outcomes for grade five language arts, aspects would be numbered as follows:

1. Language Arts (Reading Comprehension)
1.1 "demonstrate understanding of the main ideas or events" (BC Ministry of Education, 1996a, p. 80)
1.2 "extend understanding of a given selection by developing related questions and activities" (p. 80)
1.3 "use a variety of written and graphic forms… to organize details and information" (p. 80)
1.4 "identify the literary elements, including setting, plot, climax, and conflict, in a given selection" (p. 80)

To differentiate between core aspects (mandatory) and choice aspects (optional), the graduation document denotes ".1" as core, and subsequent numbers as choice (i.e., .2, .3, etc.). Accordingly, the 1.1 aspect in the example above is mandatory and must be completed to receive portfolio program credit, whereas 1.2 to 1.4 are choice aspects.

Including a core component "ensures that all students are able to achieve a minimum provincial standard in Graduation Portfolio" (BC Ministry of Education, 2004, p. 103). A checklist format outlines the criteria for the graduation portfolio core. "Portfolio Core evidence is evaluated as either complete or incomplete. Students are assigned full marks when they have addressed all aspect criteria…. There are no part marks for Portfolio Core aspects" (p. 103). All six organizers of the graduation program consist of five criteria, thereby constituting 30% of the total mark. Using these guidelines set out by the BC Ministry of Education, Table 4 illustrates a portfolio core guide based on one of the grade five reading learning outcomes listed previously. The table is outlined in a similar format as the graduation guide. Figure 10 illustrates an example of a self-reflection activity with a peer comment section to accompany this core guide.

PARENT RESPONSE SHEET FOR PORTFOLIO REVIEW
☆ ☆ ☆ ☆ ☆

Please complete this sheet after looking over this portfolio with your child.

Two Stars
Math Minutes & Math Test – We were very proud of Graison's ability and desire to set goals and reach them. He is also improving with staying on task which was shown in the volume of completed work.

Habitat Science Quiz – We were impressed with Graison's understanding of this complex subject matter. Great job!

One Wish
Our wish for Graison is to improve his printing skills. With practice, an improvement in printing will enable Graison to more effectively and efficiently put his thoughts on to paper. The example is the whole story from Set. 15/05. We have noticed a considerable improvement since this time.

Parent of a Grade 2 Student

Table 4
Example of a Portfolio Core Guide

Portfolio Core Guide	Language Arts (Reading Comprehension)
Name: _____ Date: _____ Teacher: _____ 3 Marks: _____ ☆ ☆ ☆	Aspect 1.1 **Demonstrate understanding of main ideas and events**
Portfolio Quality = Action + **Reflection**	**Tips to help you create your evidence**

For demonstrating understanding of main ideas and events Your portfolio evidence must meet all three criteria. ☆ **Criteria #1** Select a work sample that demonstrates your ability to understand main ideas and events. ☆ **Criteria #2** Complete a self-reflection form. ☆ **Criteria #3** Share your work with a peer.	Criteria Check		You must meet all three criteria to receive credit for this aspect.

	Student	**Teacher**	• Subject areas to consider include language arts, social studies, and science. • Work samples to think about as an entry include the following class activities: ✓ Collecting Details and Main Ideas ✓ Chain of Events ✓ Five W's ✓ E-Chart ✓ Time Line ✓ Spider Map ✓ Venn Diagram • A self-reflection form with a peer comment section will be provided.

Format adapted from BC Ministry of Education, 2004, p. 11.

Figure 10. Self-reflection activity to accompany core guide.

SELF-REFLECTION

Name: _____   Date: _____

Select the work sample that you feel best meets the core guide criteria of understanding main ideas and events. List some skills or strategies that you used to complete the activity:

_____

_____

_____

_____

I would like others to notice...

_____

_____

_____

Peer Comment: I especially like...

- _____

    _____

- _____

    _____

Student Signature: _____

Peer Signature: _____

In following this handbook, the transition to using the portfolio core guide presented in Table 4 should prove to be smooth and productive. Students have experience with all of the elements outlined in the guide including following criteria, self-reflection, and peer evaluation. As with any assignment, teachers need to discuss the criteria and corresponding activities with the class.

Credit earned from the portfolio core aspects and the presentation component outlined in the BC graduation portfolio program comprise 50% of the total mark, which constitutes the minimal score required to graduate. Choice aspects allow students to "choose areas in which they want to submit Portfolio Choice evidence for up to 50% of the Graduation Portfolio mark" (BC Ministry of Education, 2004, p. 3). In essence, students complete as few or as many aspects as they wish (BC Ministry of Education, 2005).

Once again, this component of the graduation portfolio program can be modified in a variety of ways to include learning outcomes at any grade level and provide students with choice experiences. Including choice items encourages students to select aspects that interest them as well as expand their knowledge and skills introduced in the core guides (2005). To illustrate, consider the following reading comprehension learning outcome: It is expected that students will "extend their understanding of a given selection by developing related questions and activities" (BC Ministry of Education, 1996a, p. 80). Following the format and guidelines set out in the graduation program, Table 5 presents a portfolio choice guide.

Student worksheets listed in Table 4 can be accessed at the following web sites:

Houghton Mifflin
http://www.eduplace.com/graphicorganizer/

edHelper.com
http://www.edhelper.com/teachers/graphic_organizers.htm

**STUDENT RESPONSE SHEET
FOR PORTFOLIO REVIEW**
☆☆☆☆☆

Name: Austin
Date: Oct. 25, 2005

Two Stars -- What I do well.
I do well in Language Arts because it is fun.

I do well in gym.

One Wish -- What I can improve.
I can improve my reading.

**Action Plan –
What I can do to improve.**
I can improve that I can be better at reading with expression.

Grade 2 Work Sample

Table 5
Example of a Portfolio Choice Guide

Portfolio Choice Guide Name: _____ Date: _____ Teacher: _____ Mark: _____ / 5 ☆ ☆ ☆ ☆ ☆	Language Arts (Reading Comprehension) Aspect 1.2 **Extend understanding of a given selection by developing related questions and activities**

Portfolio Quality = Action + Reflection				**Tips to help you create your evidence**
☆ ☆ ☆ Generate seven questions based on a reading passage. **Evidence meets three criteria** Two or three must be literal or detail type questions (i.e., answers are found in the text). Two or three need to be inferential type questions (i.e., answers involve using text to read "between the lines"). Two or three should be critical type questions (i.e., answers involve using the text to formulate an opinion or reaction). **Criteria Check** ☐ ☐ ☐	☆ Choose or create an extended activity. **Evidence meets one more criteria** Complete an extended activity suitable for the reading passage. **Criteria Check** ☐	☆ Share your work with a peer. **Evidence meets one more criteria** Share the questions and extended activity with a peer. Complete a self-reflection form. **Criteria Check** ☐	**Mark** **/ 5**	◆ Reading passages can include a story or novel as well as sections or chapters from social studies and science texts. ◆ Refer to the handout for examples of literal, inferential, and critical type question stems. ◆ Choose an extended activity from the list posted in the classroom. Examples of activities include: • creating a new ending • completing a book review • timeline of events • designing a crossword puzzle etc. or ◆ Create your own extended activity such as a board game. ◆ A self-reflection form with a peer comment section will be provided.

Format adapted from BC Ministry of Education, 2004, p. 27.

As set out in the BC graduation program, evaluation of portfolio choice evidence differs from that of core aspects in that "students can earn up to 5 marks for each [choice] aspect, depending on the quality and extent of their effort" (BC Ministry of Education, 2004, p. 24). The portfolio process is such that teachers have much flexibility at the elementary, middle, and junior secondary levels to establish their own assessment guidelines to deliver learning outcome requirements. In reference to the choice guide presented in Table 5, for example, teachers could request that students select three of the five criteria to complete; thereby fulfilling learning outcome expectations as well as providing students with choice. Another option is to require that students complete a given number of criteria from among all of the choice aspects. To illustrate, consider once again the following reading comprehension choice aspects (BC Ministry of Education, 1996a, p. 80): (1.2) "extend understanding of a given selection by developing related questions and activities;" (1.3) "use a variety of written and graphic forms to organize details and information;" and (1.4) "identify the literary elements, including setting, plot, climax, and conflict, in a given selection." Providing that each aspect consists of five criteria, totaling 15 in all, requirements could comprise of 10 choice items in addition to the three core criteria outlined in Table 4. Appendix G presents the reading organizer in its entirety including the core aspect and three choice aspects.

Integrating Thinking Skills

Another way to create criteria is to integrate thinking skills into learning experiences. Bloom's Taxonomy and Gardner's Multiple Intelligences provide an opportunity to use levels and methods as the basis for collecting portfolio evidence. Consider the following six levels of Bloom's Taxonomy for the cognitive domain of learning ("Bloom's Taxonomy," n.d., ¶ 3):

Knowledge: remembering or recalling appropriate, previously learned information to draw out factual (usually right or wrong) answers.

Comprehension: grasping or understanding the meaning of informational materials.

Student Self-Reflection

Name: Quinn
Date: October 24th

Work Sample:
Mad Minute Booklet

This piece of work makes me feel a little bit sad and a little bit good because... I really need to improve on my mad minutes. I think that I just need to set my goals a little bit lower and I need to lower my temper about how I do on my mad minutes. But I am really proud about how I did.

Somethink that I still need to work on is: My adding and subtracting, and watching for the signs.

Signature: Quinn

Grade 2 Work Sample

View the BC *Graduation Portfolio Assessment and Focus Areas: A program Guide* at http://www.bced.gov.bc.ca/graduation/portfolio/moe_grad_portfolio_p1_p2.pdf.

Application: applying previously learned information (or knowledge) to new and unfamiliar situations.

Analysis: breaking down information into parts, or examining (and trying to understand the organizational structure of) information.

Synthesis: applying prior knowledge and skills to combine elements into a pattern not clearly there before.

Evaluation: judging or deciding according to some set of criteria, without real right or wrong answers.

Ways to use Bloom's Taxonomy include creating an organizer using the six levels as core and choice aspects (see Table 6). Another option is to integrate thinking skills into organizers such as language arts, science, and mathematics. Choice aspects 1.2 to 1.4 in Appendix G incorporates higher level thinking skills including analysis (e.g., compare and infer), synthesis (e.g., create and design), and evaluation (e.g., justify and support).

Likewise, the following Gardner's Multiple Intelligences provide another method of establishing portfolio criteria: verbal/linguistic, logical/mathematical, visual/spatial, body/kinesthetic, musical/rhythmic, interpersonal, intrapersonal, and the naturalist. Table 7 presents the body/kinesthetic intelligence as a choice aspect.

Using learning outcomes and thinking skills for portfolio organization demonstrates some of the many possibilities that exist for teachers. Portfolio evidence becomes a matter of examining existing curriculum and instructional strategies to integrate into the portfolio process. As mentioned previously, the portfolio process is non-linear in nature and takes as many different paths as the creative mind will permit.

Visit the *Theory into Practice* (TIP) database for more information on Bloom's Taxonomies and Gardner's Multiple Intelligences:
http://tip.psychology.org/theories.html

**STUDENT RESPONSE SHEET
FOR PORTFOLIO REVIEW**

Name: Shauntay
Date: Oct. 25th

Two Stars -- What I do well.
I'm good at math.

I'm good at gym. I love gym.

**One Wish –
What I can improve.**
I want to be a better listener.

**Action Plan –
What I can do to improve.**
I can try not to talk in classes.

Grade 2 Work Sample

Table 6
Using Bloom's Taxonomy for Portfolio Criteria

Portfolio Choice Guide				Bloom's Taxonomy: Analysis
Name: _____ Date: _____ Teacher: _____ Mark: _____ / 5 ☆☆☆☆☆				Aspect _____ **Breaking information into parts**
Portfolio Quality = Action + Reflection				**Tips to help you create your evidence**
☆☆☆ Demonstrate analysis ability. **Evidence meets three criteria** Select a work sample that demonstrates your analysis ability. Describe how the activity was broken down into parts. List the skills used for the analysis (e.g., comparing, examining, categorizing, etc.). **Criteria Check** ☐ ☐ ☐	☆ Reflect on the entry. **Evidence meets one more criteria** Choose a self-reflection form to include with the analysis. **Criteria Check** ☐	☆ Share work with a parent/adult. **Evidence meets one more criteria** Share your work with a parent or other adult. Provide the reviewer with a response sheet to fill in. **Criteria Check** ☐	 **Mark** **/ 5**	♦ Words associated with breaking information into parts include the following: appraise, calculate, explain, separate, categorize, classify, arrange, compare, contrast, differentiate, experiment, examine, discriminate, inventory, question, and test. ♦ Subject areas to consider for evidence include language arts, mathematics, social studies, and science. ♦ Work samples to think about as an entry include the following class activities: • Venn Diagram • Story Map • Scientific Method Summary • Problem Solving • Graphs • Time Line • Cause/Effect • Chain of Events • Webs • Topic/Main Ideas • 5 W's ♦ Self-reflection forms and a reviewer response sheet will be provided.

Format adapted from BC Ministry of Education, 2004, p. 27.

Table 7

Using Gardner's Multiple Intelligences for Portfolio Criteria

Portfolio Choice Guide				Gardner's Multiple Intelligences: Body/Kinesthetic Intelligence
Name: _____ Date: _____ Teacher: _____ Mark: _____ / 5 ☆☆☆☆☆				Aspect _____ **Demonstrating the ability to learn by using body movements**
Portfolio Quality = Action + Reflection				**Tips to help you create your evidence**
☆☆☆ Demonstrate the body/kinesthetic multiple intelligence. **Evidence meets three criteria** Select a work sample, product, or performance that demonstrates the body/kinesthetic intelligence. Describe how the activity relates to this intelligence. List the skills used for the intelligence (e.g., constructing, performing, moving, designing, stretching, folding, twisting, etc.). **Criteria Check** ☐ ☐ ☐	☆ Reflect on the entry. **Evidence meets one more criteria** Choose a self-reflection form to include with the evidence. **Criteria Check** ☐	☆ Share work with a parent/adult. **Evidence meets one more criteria** Share your work with a parent or other adult. Provide the reviewer with a response sheet to fill in. **Criteria Check** ☐	**Mark** / 5	◆ Intelligence Characteristics ("Kinesthetic," 2006, ¶ 1): Sensory – internalizes information through bodily sensation Reflexive – responds quickly and intuitively to physical stimulus Tactile – demonstrates well-developed gross and/or fine motor skills Concrete – expresses feelings and ideas through body movement Coordinated – shows dexterity, agility, flexibility, balance and poise Task Orientated – strive to learn by doing ◆ Evidence to think about include the following class or home/community activities: ▪ Sports (e.g., game, karate, gymnastics routine, exercises) ▪ Drama (e.g., skit, play, re-enactment, mime, role play) ▪ Dance ▪ Hands-on learning (e.g., using manipulatives, keyboarding, science experiment, building or constructing, interactive games) ◆ Self-reflection forms and a reviewer response sheet will be provided.

Format adapted from BC Ministry of Education, 2004, p. 27.

Graduation Portfolio Subjects

Another framework to consider in transitioning students to a graduation portfolio program is using corresponding subjects or organizers. Again, using the BC graduation program as an example, Table 8 illustrates curriculum subject areas of the graduation program that align with those of other grades.

Table 8
Aligning Graduation Portfolio Subjects with Other Grade Levels

Graduation Portfolio Program Subject Areas Grades 10 – 12	Corresponding Curriculum Subject Areas
Arts and Design	Fines Arts (Grades K – 12)
Education and Career Planning	Personal Planning: Career Development (Grades K – 7) Health and Career Education (Grades 8 – 9) Career and Personal Planning (Grades 8 – 12)
Employability Skills	Personal Planning: Career Development (Grades K – 7) Career and Personal Planning: Career Development (Grades 8 – 12)
Information Technology	Information Technology (Grades 8 – 12)
Personal Health	Physical Education (Grades K – 7) Personal Planning: Personal Development (Grades K – 7) Health and Career Education (Grades 8 – 9) Career and Personal Planning: Personal Development (Grades 8 – 12)

In addition to specific curriculum areas that align with the graduation program as indicated in Table 8, learning outcomes from other subjects overlap. For example, although Information Technology is not a subject per se in the elementary grades, using electronic sources for information and communication as well as data analysis is stated in many learning outcomes for Language Arts and Mathematics.

Using corresponding subject areas as the foundation for the portfolio process can be introduced at any grade level. Additionally, including artwork, computer-generated application products, or physical education evidence as part of best work and growth portfolios is another way to incorporate elements of graduation portfolio curriculum requirements.

Scope and Sequence

Aligning graduation portfolio programs with earlier grades provides educators with a foundation to develop a scope and sequence chart. Scope and sequence is defined as "a curriculum plan, usually in chart form, in which a range of instructional objectives, skills, etc., is organized according to the successive levels at which they are taught" ("Nebraska K - 12," 1999, p. 6). Such a chart can be organized by portfolio components that outline expectations for each grade level. This provides teachers with a framework to introduce and extend portfolio skills in a sequential manner that builds on previous knowledge and skills which, ultimately, lead to a successful graduation portfolio program. Following are some suggestions for establishing a school-wide scope and sequence chart at the elementary, middle, and junior secondary levels:

- begin with the scope in mind: the vision of students meeting the graduation program requirements
- establish a template for the scope and sequence chart (see Table 9 for an example)
- make available any learning outcomes or standards set by district and province or state levels that are associated with the portfolio process (refer to Appendix H)
- prepare copies of existing portfolio benchmarks to serve as examples
- form a primary committee consisting of a teacher from each grade level to create a draft copy of the scope and sequence chart
- form an intermediate committee (e.g., grades four to seven) also consisting of a teacher from each grade level; use the primary draft to continue the scope and sequence chart
- examine the draft scope and sequence chart in grade groups; all kindergarten and grade one teachers meet together to examine each component of the chart to ensure that their grade level consists of age appropriate and the necessary prerequisite skills; grade one teachers then meet with all the grade two teachers to examine the grade one and two chart; etc.
- make revisions based on grade group recommendations

PARENT RESPONSE SHEET FOR PORTFOLIO REVIEW
☆ ☆ ☆ ☆ ☆

Please complete this sheet after looking over this portfolio with your child.

Two Stars
Spelling-practicing every day and doing well on tests. Way to focus, Reese!

Math Test-You did very well. Keep up the great work!

One Wish
Expand on your writing. I know that you can do it. Remember, you need a good beginning, middle and end.

Parent of a Grade 2 Student

Student Self-Reflection

Name: Graison
Date: October 25th

Work Sample: My Mad Minute

This piece of work makes me feel happy **because...** I got the most on my mad minute.

Somethink that I still need to work on is:
Staying on task longer, and setting higher goals and trying to reach them.

Signature: Graison

Grade 2 Work Sample

- look at the benchmarks in their entirety as a staff for any further input and final touches
- middle or junior secondary school staff continue the scope and sequence chart in the same manner

Developing a scope and sequence chart is a collaborative team effort that results in continuous and successful learning. "As students gain more and more experience with the skills and activities involved in keeping… [p]ortfolios, they'll gain in ability to take more responsibility for many parts of the process" (Frank, 1994, p. 102). In this light, scope and sequence charts can be revisited each year for revisions and modifications. Appendix H provides a scope and sequence chart using portfolio components presented in this handbook along with BC learning outcomes.

Table 9

Template Sample for Scope and Sequence Chart

GRADE LEVEL:	LEARNING OUTCOMES/ STANDARDS
Purpose/ Type	
Subject(s)/ Curriculum Area(s)	
Audience	
Criteria	
Selection Process	
Time Frame	
Self-Reflection	
Goal Setting	
Presentation	
Graduation Program	

Section V:
Sharing the Portfolio

By the nature of the purposes of portfolios -- to *show* growth, to *show*case excellence -- portfolios are meant to be shared. The samples, reflections and other contents allow or invite others to observe and celebrate students' progress and accomplishments. A portfolio should tell a story, and that story should be told. (Mueller, 2003a, p. 12)

The portfolio process becomes more meaningful when students have an opportunity to share their learning experiences with others. As students prepare to communicate their story to an audience, they further their understanding of themselves as learners. Preparing students to present their portfolios relates back to decisions regarding the audience and criteria for portfolios as a whole.

Teachers and Students as the Audience

A school setting offers a variety of audiences for students to present their portfolios. Classmates as well as students and teachers from other grades provide a starting point for students to practice, receive feedback, and benefit from observing other presentations. A class discussion as to potential audiences promotes student involvement and may include the following:

- teacher (conference format)
- a peer or small group
- class as a whole
- buddies
- another class completing portfolios
- students from a secondary school who are working on graduation portfolios

Sharing work with others is always an occasion for students to receive feedback. Written feedback suits smaller audiences whereas it is more practical for an entire class to give verbal

---

PARENT RESPONSE SHEET FOR PORTFOLIO REVIEW
☆ ☆ ☆ ☆ ☆

Please complete this sheet after looking over this portfolio with your child.

Two Stars
Jayden, we are very proud of your Thanksgiving piece. Your printing and spelling are very good.

We are happy that you are thankful for good things. We have raised a very thoughtful little boy.

One Wish
We talked about your Elephant test and how all the answers were right in the story. You need to remember to take your time and read things very carefully. Keep working hard!

Parent of a Grade 2 Student

"Portfolios are a terrific way of communicating with parents and providing a 'heads-up' before reporting periods. They are also a way for the child to see the parent(s) and teacher working as a team in their learning as both the parent(s) and teacher offer feedback on their work."

Nicole Person, Grade 2 Teacher

feedback. To assist viewers in formulating responses to presentations, the following prompts promote positive and constructive feedback:

- My favourite/most enjoyable part of your presentation is….
- I really like….
- I am very impressed with….
- Your portfolio reveals the following about you as a learner….
- You have shown great improvement/growth in….
- What surprised me from your presentation is….
- An idea that occurred to me during your presentation is….
- I could really relate to….
- From your presentation, I learned….
- A question that I have is…
- Please explain in more detail….
- A suggestion to improve your presentation is….

These prompts also provide a framework for designing response forms as illustrated in Figure 11.

Figure 11. Viewer response form.

Dear Reviewer,

Thank you for looking at my portfolio with me. Your feedback is important and valuable to me as a learner. Please use any of the following prompts to comment on my presentation:

- My favourite/most enjoyable part of your presentation is….
- I really like….
- I am very impressed with….
- Your portfolio reveals the following about you as a learner….
- You have shown great improvement/growth in….
- What surprised me from your presentation is….
- An idea that occurred to me during your presentation is….
- I could really relate to….
- From your presentation, I learned….
- A question that I have is…
- Please explain in more detail….
- A suggestion to improve your presentation is….

Comments:

_____

_____

Thank you for taking the time to respond to my portfolio.

Sincerely,

_____

Reviewer: _____   Date: _____

Parents as the Audience

A school year consists of many events and occasions to share portfolios with parents including open houses, formal and informal reporting periods, parent/teacher conferences, and student-led conferences.

Open house. Many schools host an open house early in the school year. This is an opportune time for teachers and students to inform parents about portfolios and how they can support their child with the process. Newsletters or brochures outlining the purpose of portfolios and information as to when portfolios will be shared with families are ideal to distribute at an open house.

Formal reporting. Teachers may want to consider sending portfolios along with formal report cards. Portfolios serve to compliment information outlined in the report card with evidence of student learning. Supplementing report cards with portfolios provides a more comprehensive profile of a student's learning and progress.

Informal reporting. In BC, schools are required to provide two informal reports each year. "Informal reporting is the ongoing communication between parents and teachers that occurs throughout the school year. Informal reports may include telephone conferences, interim reports, written communication, portfolio reviews and face-to-face conferences" (BC Ministry of Education, 2001, p. 36). Many schools hold parent/teacher conferences and/or student-led conferences. Some schools conduct a conference for one informal reporting session and send written communication home for the other report. Regardless of the reporting method, portfolios serve as the focal point for sharing and demonstrating student learning. Additionally, such occasions enable parents to provide feedback on their child's portfolio.

Parent/teacher conferences. Portfolios provide "teachers with a built-in system for planning parent-teacher conferences. With the portfolio as the basis for discussion, the teacher and parent can review concrete examples of the child's work, rather than trying to discuss the child's progress in the abstract" (Grace, 1992, ¶ 15). Furthermore, portfolios clearly communicate a student's learning experiences in a face-to-face setting with the teacher, parents, and student.

For more information on parent/teacher and student-led conferences, read:

Reporting Student Progress: Policy and Practice (Informal Reporting section) at the BC Ministry of Education web site:
http://www.bced.gov.bc.ca/reportcards/reporting_student_progress.pdf

Student-Led Conferences: A Growing Trend at Education World:
http://www.educationworld.com/a_admin/admin/admin112.shtml

Student-led conferences. "A student-led parent/teacher conference provides an opportunity for students to evaluate their progress and lead a reporting conference" (BC Primary Teachers' Association, 1992, p. 10.53). This is a prime setting for students to tell the story of their learning. Portfolios provide the basis for sharing and discussing student achievements, strengths, areas requiring improvement, and goals for further learning.

Special Portfolio Events

As a culminating event to the portfolio process, teachers and students may choose to host a special event for presenting portfolios. An afternoon tea sets a pleasant atmosphere for students to share portfolios with families. Likewise, a portfolio evening adds an element of excitement and importance to the portfolio presentation. Such endeavors empower students to play an integral role in the planning and organization including designing invitations, decorating the classroom, selecting background music, and arranging beverages and snacks for the guests. Additionally, classes have access to school resources to demonstrate individual and group activities related to subject areas such as physical education, technology, and music. As well, three-dimensional projects and products can be displayed for all viewers to enjoy. These occasions also allow teachers and students to extend invitations to community members, next year's teachers, and educators who are interested in implementing the portfolio process.

Revisiting Portfolio Criteria

As outlined in the *Criteria and Selection Process* portion of Section II, criteria and examples of portfolios are shared with students at the onset of the process to enable them to foster a vision of the final product. It now becomes a matter of revisiting these criteria. Since students have been selecting entries during the time frame set by the teacher, this criterion outlined in the checklist or rubric will have been met (i.e., number of entries, reflection sheets, and dated work). Another criterion most likely completed by this stage is the title or cover page. Remaining criteria, such as a letter to

---

Student Self-Reflection

Name: Shanelle
Date: Oct. 24, 2005

Work Sample: Math

This piece of work makes me feel happy **because...** I did my best. I need to do better. I need to practice my adding.

Something that I still need to work on is:
2 numbers by 2 adding in math

Signature: Shanelle

Grade 2 Work Sample

My favourite part of the portfolio process is...

"I get to bring it home and I get to have a portfolio party."

"bringing it home and sharing with my parents."

"drawing a picture of myself."

"The best thing about the portfolio is to learn."

"I get to read my portfolio at bed time."

"I like showing my parents how proud of my work I am and having the snack."

Grade 2 Students

viewers or an introductory letter and table of contents, become part of the preparation to present the portfolio.

Letter to viewers/Introductory letter. Letters to viewers or introductory letters provide an audience with information as to the purpose of the portfolio. Additionally, it is an opportunity for students to reflect on the portfolio process itself. Including student input into the contents of the letter is necessary in order for students to capture the essence of their learning journey. A class brainstorming session to produce question stems and prompts will provide the structure for the letter. Following are some possibilities:

- What is the purpose of your portfolio?
- What new things did you learn about yourself from doing a portfolio?
- What does your portfolio tell us about you as a learner?
- Describe how your _____ (reading, writing, mathematics, art, etc.) skills have improved since September.
- What do you want viewers to notice most about your portfolio?
- What is your favourite part of the portfolio process? Which part of the portfolio process did you find challenging? How can the portfolio process be improved?
- How has your ability to self-reflect changed or improved throughout the year?
- How have the following helped you as a learner?
  - ✓ self-reflection
  - ✓ rubrics and checklists
  - ✓ feedback from teachers, peers, and parents
  - ✓ sharing your portfolio
- What are your strengths as a learner? What are some areas to focus on for improvement?
- List some learning goals for the future. Describe how your teacher, peers, and parents can assist you in achieving your goals.
- Next time you start a new portfolio, what might you do differently?
- What advice or helpful suggestions would you give someone just beginning a portfolio?

Following the brainstorming session, a discussion as to which prompts are deemed essential will ensure that viewers

"Next time I start a portfolio I will put my stuff from my lowest mark to my highest mark in all of the subjects I have, and my worst writing to my best writing."

Grade 5 Student

Grade 2 Students Reflect on the Portfolio Process

What new things did you learn about yourself from doing a portfolio? What else have you learned from the portfolio process?

"I got better at lots of work like my mad minute and my listening sheet. I learned that I have to try my best."

"How to read with fluency and I got better at math. I've also learned about to write better."

"I realized that I did better on my mad minutes. I also improved in gym."

"That I need to improve on Science. I didn't know that I was so good at math."

"I got better at reading. I need to work on printing."

understand and appreciate the intent of the portfolio process from the perspective of the students. For example, the class may reach a consensus that the purpose of the portfolio and what each student learned from the process should be part of the introductory letter. Allowing students to choose additional questions and prompts from the list will enable students to personalize and add meaning to the story of their learning.

A structured prompt and question format will assist students in the younger grades in composing a letter. Figure 12 provides an example of a template.

> "I learned [from doing a portfolio] that I can do times tables really fast, my work is getting neater and my paragraphing is getting more interesting."
>
> Grade 5 Student

Figure 12. Example of an introductory letter.

MY PORTFOLIO: LETTER OF INTRODUCTION

Name: _____   Grade: _____

Teacher: _____   Date: _____

Purpose of Portfolio:

_____

_____

I would like you to notice:

_____

_____

I have learned the following things from doing a portfolio:

_____

_____

Some learning goals for the future are:

_____

_____

Thank you for looking at my portfolio with me.

Sincerely,

_____

Table of contents. Including a table of contents provides an opportunity for students to organize portfolio items that also serves as an agenda for presentations. Guidelines for students to arrange portfolio materials relate to the purpose. Growth portfolios, for instance, suit a chronological system of earlier and later work. In reference to the reading portfolio outlined in Appendix G, ordering the entries by aspects is appropriate (i.e., aspect 1.1, 1.2, 1.3, and 1.4). Students' insight into how they would like viewers to follow and understand their learning journey is another important factor to consider when designing a table of contents. As an example, some students may want to begin their portfolios with an accomplished piece of writing that is followed by earlier samples depicting the progression to their present status as a writer. Other students might wish to begin with work that demonstrates meaningful, satisfying, best effort, most favourite, greatest improvement, or challenging entries. A further consideration for a table of contents includes the dates of each item (see Figure 13).

As with all stages of the portfolio process, students further their understanding when teachers use their own portfolio contents to model composing an introductory letter and table of contents. Since presentations may occur at intervals throughout the year and involve different audiences as well as varying developmental levels of the portfolio process, teachers can also model how they would update and revise their introductory letter and table of contents.

"All about me" themes and name projects add a fun and personal touch to student portfolios. Visit the following web sites to access some activities:

About Me at edHelper
http://www.edhelper.com/clipart/teachers/bs-aboutme1.pdf

All About Me at abcteach
http://www.abcteach.com/free/members/12174.pdf

Name Project at abcteach
http://www.abcteach.com/Backtoschool/name.htm

Figure 13. Example of a table of contents.

My Writing Portfolio
By Jane Smith, Grade 3

Table of Contents

Letter of Introduction	December 2005
Poem: Fall Cinquain with a Self-reflection Form	September 2005
Writing Snapshot Assessment with Rubric and a Goal Setting Sheet	September 2005
Photo: Sharing my Writing with our Buddies	October 2005
Halloween Paragraph: Rough Draft and Final Copy/ Self-reflection with Teacher and Peer Feedback	October 2005
Two Journal Entries with Self-reflection Form	November 2005
Writing from Another Subject: Book Report	November 2005
Prewriting Web: Letter to Santa	December 2005
Writing Pieces to Keep at Home	Sept.-Dec. 2005
Parent Response Sheet (Two Stars and One Wish) → Return to School with Portfolio	
Next Portfolio Presentation (Student-led Conferences)	March 2006

Practicing the Presentation

Once students have completed the introductory letter and table of contents, they are now prepared to practice their presentation. The listener and speaker points outlined in Appendix F, *Working with Others Poster*, also apply to presentations as illustrated below:

Listeners need to remember to:

- focus attention on the speaker/presenter
- wait for your turn to talk
- ask a question or make a comment that shows you listened
- give the speaker a compliment or describe something that you liked about his/her work
- show respect by encouraging and supporting the ideas of your partner or others in your group
- fill out any forms handed out for the activity

Speakers need to remember to:

- present information in a logical order so the audience can follow along
- talk clearly with appropriate volume so your partner or group members can hear
- keep eye contact with the audience
- be prepared to answer questions
- show courteousness by thanking the participant(s) for listening and sharing comments/questions

Teachers begin by modeling the presentation using their own portfolios. Referring to the criteria above and the prompts outlined in Figure 11, students then provide verbal feedback to the teacher's presentation. Practicing individually and then with a peer or small group helps students gain confidence to enjoy and celebrate the story of their learning.

My favourite part of the portfolio process is...

"My favourite part of the portfolio process was my 'all about me' paragraph because I love to type and because I can look back on what I was like when I am in grade six."

"My favourite part of the portfolio process is the book report because it was fun to make the tape and take it home to listen to!"

"My favourite part of the portfolio process was my Terry Fox story because I learned more about him and why he was a Canadian hero."

"My favourite part of the portfolio process is the 'all about me' because when I look back on it I'll see how much I've changed. It was also lots of fun answering the questions."

"My favourite part of the portfolio process was my mad minutes because I am achieving on it."

"My favourite part of the portfolio process was making the [book report] tape because you can keep it forever and look back."

Grade 5 Students

Section VI: Final Words

Begin Small

At the start, remember that the focus is on the portfolio process so begin small and simple. Once teachers feel comfortable with the process, more variety and encompassing elements of the types of portfolios, student choice, peer involvement, and self-reflection activities can be introduced.

Plan Ahead

Use the *Planning Outline Summary* (Table 2) and the *Teacher Portfolio Planning Form* (Figure 6) to plan and make decisions regarding the following key components of the portfolio process:

- purpose/type of portfolio
- curriculum area(s) and portfolio content
- audience
- criteria
- selection process
- organization and storage system
- time frame
- self-reflection and goal setting activities
- sharing and presenting the portfolio

Engage Students

Try to involve students as much as possible in decisions relating to key elements such as establishing criteria, selection of entries, potential audiences, introductory letters, organizing portfolio content, and planning special portfolio events. Such involvement will ensure an accurate and personalized story of the students' learning. Think of the teacher's role as that of a facilitator to guide and encourage student development and ownership of the portfolio.

Anything Goes

Portfolios are non-linear in nature, which means that "anything goes." There is no one best way to implement portfolios in the classroom. Remember to examine and use current curriculum practices and activities to shape portfolios.

Model the Process

Adhere to the old adage, "practice what you preach." Develop a teaching portfolio along with the class to model the various elements of the process. For more information on teaching portfolios, refer to *Preparing a Teaching Portfolio* at <http://www.utexas.edu/academic/cte/teachfolio.html> and *Teaching and Academic Growth* (TAG) at <http://www.tag.ubc.ca/resources/teachingportfolios/eportfolios/>.

Involve Parents

Communicate with parents early on in the portfolio process. Parents serve as a valuable resource to support their child's learning through portfolios.

Community of Learners

Collaborating and working as a team with colleagues to implement portfolios is what the teaching profession is all about. Sharing ideas and insights will contribute to a successful and enjoyable portfolio experience. Additionally, discuss portfolios with students and parents to seek their input into the program's strengths as well as how the process can be improved.

References

Andersen, G. (n.d.). *Portfolio assessment of your work: A guide.* Retrieved August 27, 2005, from http://www.kckps.k12.ks.us/course/portfol.html

Arter, J., & McTighe, J. (2001). *Scoring rubrics in the classroom.* Thousand Oaks, California: Corwin Press Inc.

Authentic assessment. (n.d.). Retrieved August 4, 2005, from the Funderstanding Web site: http://www.funderstanding.com/authentic_assessment.cfm

Bloom's taxonomy: An overview. (n.d.). Retrieved January 24, 2006, from http://www.teachervision.fen.com/page/2171.html

British Columbia Ministry of Education. (1994, February). *Portfolio assessment.* Victoria, British Columbia, Canada: Ministry of Education, Curriculum Development Branch.

British Columbia Ministry of Education. (1996). *English language arts K to 7: Integrated resource package.* Victoria, British Columbia, Canada: Ministry of Education, Skills and Training Department.

British Columbia Ministry of Education. (1996). *English language arts 8 to 10: Integrated resource package* (appendix section). Retrieved February 15, 2006, from the British Columbia Ministry of Education Web site: http://www.bced.gov.bc.ca/irp/ela810/apa.htm

British Columbia Ministry of Education. (1997). *Career and personal planning 8 to 12: Integrated resource package* (appendix section). Retrieved February 16, 2006, from the British Columbia Ministry of Education Web site: http://www.bced.gov.bc.ca/irp/capp/apa.htm

British Columbia Ministry of Education. (1999). *Personal planning K to 7: Integrated resource package.* Retrieved August 4, 2005, from the British Columbia Ministry of Education Web site: http://www.bced.gov.bc.ca/irp/pp/pptoc.htm

British Columbia Ministry of Education. (2000, February). *BC performance standards. Writing.* Victoria, British Columbia, Canada: Student Assessment and Program Evaluation Branch.

British Columbia Ministry of Education. (2001). *Reporting student progress: Policy and practice.* Retrieved February 10, 2006, from the British Columbia Ministry of Education Web site: http://www.bced.gov.bc.ca/reportcards/reporting_student_progress.pdf

British Columbia Ministry of Education. (2004). *Graduation portfolio assessment and focus areas: A program guide.* Retrieved July 11, 2005, from the British Columbia Ministry of Education Web site: http://www.bced.gov.bc.ca/graduation/portfolio/moe_grad_portfolio_p1_p2.pdf

British Columbia Ministry of Education. (2005). *Graduation portfolio for families.* Retrieved October 14, 2005, from the British Columbia Ministry of Education Web site: http://www.bced.gov.bc.ca/graduation/portfolio/gradportfam_2005.pdf

British Columbia Primary Teachers' Association. (1992). *Evaluation techniques and resources: Book II.* Vancouver, British Columbia, Canada: BC Primary Teachers' Association.

Chappuis, Jan. (2005, November). Helping students understand assessment. *Educational Leadership, 63*(3), 44-47.

Crandall, J., Jaramillo, A., Olsen, L., & Peyton, K. (2002). Diverse teaching strategies for immigrant children. In R. W. Cole (Ed.), *More strategies for educating everybody's children* (pp. 33-71). Alexandria, Virginia: Association for Supervision and Curriculum Development.

Davies, Anne. (2000). *Making classroom assessment work.* Courtenay, British Columbia, Canada: Connections Publishing.

Davies, Anne. (2000, February). Seeing the results for yourself: A portfolio primer. *Classroom Leadership*, 3(5), 4-5.

Fiderer, A. (1999). *40 rubrics & checklists to assess reading and writing.* New York: Scholastic Professional Books.

Frank, M. (1994). *Using writing portfolios to enhance instruction & assessment.* Nashville, Tennessee: Incentive Publications, Inc.

Frank, M. (1995). *If you're trying to teach kids how to write, you've gotta have this book* (Rev. ed.). Nashville, Tennessee: Incentive Publications, Inc.

Grace, Cathy. (1992). *The portfolio and its use: Developmentally appropriate assessment of young children.* Urbana, Ill: Elementary and Early Childhood Education. (ERIC Document Reproduction Service No. ED351150)

Hampton, S. (1995). Strategies for increasing achievement in writing. In R. W. Cole (Ed.), *Educating everybody's children: Diverse teaching strategies for diverse learners* (pp. 99-120). Alexandria, VA: Association for Supervision and Curriculum Development.

Kinesthetic. (2006). Retrieved January 27, 2006, from http://surfaquarium.com/MI/profiles/kinesthetic.htm

Kline, L. (1995). A baker's dozen: Effective instructional strategies. In R. W. Cole (Ed.), *Educating everybody's children: Diverse teaching strategies for diverse learners* (pp. 21-45). Alexandria, VA: Association for Supervision and Curriculum Development.

Leahy, S., Lyon, C., Thompson, M, & William, D. (2005, November). Classroom assessment minute by minute, day by day. *Educational Leadership, 63*(3), 10-17.

Marzano, R., Pickering, D., & Pollock, J. (2001). *Classroom instruction that works: Research-based strategies for increasing student achievement.* Alexandria, Virginia: Association for Supervision and Curriculum Development.

McTighe, Jay & O'Conner, Ken. (2005, November). Seven practices for effective learning. *Educational Leadership, 63*(3), 10-17.

Meisels, S. (1997, January). Using work sampling in authentic assessments [Electronic version]. *Educational Leadership, 54*(4).

Mueller, Jon. (2003). *Portfolios.* Retrieved August 4, 2005, from the Authentic Assessment Toolbox Web site: http://jonathan.mueller.faculty.noctrl.edu/toolbox/porfolios.htm

Mueller, Jon. (2003). *Step 3: Identify the criteria for the task.* Retrieved September 20, 2005, from http://jonathan.mueller.faculty.noctrl.edu/toolbox/howstep3.htm

Nebraska K - 12 reading writing frameworks (glossary general p - t section). (1999). Retrieved January 14, 2006, from http://www.nde.state.ne.us/READ/FRAMEWORK/index2.html

Niguidula, David. (2005, November). Documenting learning with digital portfolios. *Educational Leadership, 63*(3), 44-47.

Performance criteria. (n.d.). Retrieved September 20, 2005, from the North Central Regional Educational Laboratory Web site: http://www.ncrel.org/sdrs/areas/issues/methods/assment/as8lk31.htm

Rolheiser, C., Bower, B., & Stevahn, L. (2000). *The portfolio organizer: Succeeding with portfolios in your* classroom. Alexandria, VA: Association for Supervision and Curriculum Development.

Stiggins, R. (2001). *Student-involved classroom assessment* (3rd ed.). New Jersey: Prentice-Hall, Inc.

Stiggins, R. (2002, June). Assessment crisis: The absence of assessment for learning [Electronic version]. *Phi Delta Kappan, 83*(10).

University of Phoenix (Ed.). (2002). *Lifespan development and learning* [University of Phoenix Custom Edition]. Boston: Pearson Custom Publishing.

Wilcox, John. (2006, February). Less teaching, more assessing. *Education Update, 48*(2), 1–8.

Glossaries of
Assessment and Educational Terms

Mueller's Glossary of Authentic Assessment Terms:
http://jonathan.mueller.faculty.noctrl.edu/toolbox/glossary.htm

Nebraska Department of Education Assessment Glossary:
http://www.nde.state.ne.us/READ/FRAMEWORK/glossary/assessment.html

North Central Regional Educational Laboratory (NCREL) – Glossary of
Education Terms and Acronyms:
http://www.ncrel.org/sdrs/areas/misc/glossary.htm#alternat

Teachnology: The Web Portal for Educators – Teacher Glossary of Terms in
Teaching: http://www.teach-nology.com/glossary/

Appendixes

Appendix A

Student Self-Reflection Forms

STUDENT SELF-REFLECTION

Name:_____   Date:_____

Work Sample:_____

I am selecting this entry for my portfolio because:

_____

_____

_____

_____

_____

Some things that I did to make this product my best work are:

▶ _____

▶ _____

▶ _____

Signature:_____

STUDENT SELF-REFLECTION

Name:_____ Date:_____

Work Sample:_____

I am proud of this entry that I chose for my portfolio because:

_____

_____

_____

_____

_____

Some new things that I have learned are:

▸ _____

_____

▸ _____

_____

Signature:_____

STUDENT SELF-REFLECTION

Name:_____   Date:_____

Work Sample:_____

This entry is a favourite piece of work because:

_____

_____

_____

_____

_____

I would like viewers to notice the following:

▸ _____

_____

▸ _____

_____

Signature:_____

STUDENT SELF-REFLECTION

Name:_____ Date:_____

Work Sample:_____

Some strengths of this work are:

_____

_____

_____

_____

_____

If I could continue working on this piece, I would do the following:

▶ _____

_____

▶ _____

_____

Signature:_____

STUDENT SELF-REFLECTION

Name:_____ Date:_____

Work Sample:_____

This piece of work makes me feel_____
because...

_____

_____

_____

_____

_____

Something that I still need to work on is:

_____

_____

_____

Signature:_____

STUDENT SELF-REFLECTION

Name:_____ Date:_____

Work Sample:_____

This piece of work was difficult in the following ways:

▶ _____

_____

▶ _____

_____

I overcame the difficulties or struggles by:

▶ _____

_____

▶ _____

_____

Signature:_____

STUDENT SELF-REFLECTION

Name:_____ Date:_____

Work Sample:_____

This entry shows that I am now able to do the following skill that I previously had difficulty with or could not do at all:

_____

_____

_____

_____

_____

Things that helped me learn this skill are:

▸ _____

_____

▸ _____

_____

Signature:_____

STUDENT SELF-REFLECTION

Name:_____ Date:_____

Work Sample:_____

This work shows growth and improvement in

_____

What makes this piece better than earlier work is:

▸ _____

_____

▸ _____

_____

Ways that helped me improve are:

▸ _____

_____

▸ _____

_____

Signature:_____

SELF-REFLECTION

Name:_____ Date:_____

Work Sample:_____

I am selecting this entry for my portfolio because:

_____

_____

_____

_____

What I would do differently another time is:

_____

_____

_____

_____

Signature:_____

SELF-REFLECTION

Name: _____   Date: _____

Select the work sample that you feel best meets the core guide criteria of understanding main ideas and events. List some skills or strategies that you used to complete the activity:

_____
_____
_____
_____

I would like others to notice…

_____
_____
_____

Peer Comment: I especially like…

- _____
  _____

- _____
  _____

Student Signature: _____

Peer Signature: _____

PARENT/GUARDIAN RESPONSE SHEET:
PORTFOLIO REVIEW

Dear Reviewer:

Research reveals that effective feedback identifies a learner's strengths as well as indicating areas requiring improvement. Please review your child's portfolio entries of best work. Fill in the *Two Stars* section with two positive comments about your child's progress and accomplishments. Suggest one wish that describes what you would like your child to focus on to improve his/her work.

Two Stars:

_____

_____

_____

_____

_____

_____

One Wish:

_____

_____

_____

_____

Signature of Reviewer: _____   Date: _____

Source: Adapted from Nicole Person's teacher created material. Used with permission.

Mix and Match

Many self-reflection possibilities exist by mixing and matching the prompts listed in the preceding examples. Pair the prompts in the lists below to create a variety of combinations.

I am selecting this entry for my portfolio because…	Some things that I did to make this product my best work are:
I am proud of this entry that I chose for my portfolio because…	Some new things that I have learned are:
This entry is a favourite piece of work because…	I would like viewers to notice the following:
Some strengths of this work are:	If I could continue working on this piece, I would do the following:
This piece of work makes me feel _____ because…	Something that I would do differently next time is…
This entry shows progress toward my goal of _____ in the following ways:	Something that I still need to work on is…
This piece of work was difficult in the following ways: I overcame the difficulties or struggles by:	Things that helped me learn this skill are:
This entry shows that I am now able to do the following skill that I previously had difficulty with or could not do at all:	Ways that helped me improve are:
This work shows growth and improvement in…	Explain how this entry shows improvement over an earlier piece of work.
What makes this piece better than earlier work is…	As a result of this work, a related topic or question that I am interesting in pursuing is…

Appendix B

Photo Album Activity

Photo Album Discussion

Name:_____ Date:_____

⚓ Find two or three pictures that are your favourites. Place a stickie on the page(s). Think about why these photos are your favourites.

⚓ Are there any times that you would have liked pictures taken to include in the album?

⚓ Are there any photos that you do not like? Why?

⚓ How can your photo album be improved?

⚓ What does the photo album say about you or your family?

Appendix C

Brainstorming Criteria Outline

Brainstorming Criteria

What do we need to do to produce quality or good work?

-
-
-
-
-
-

What personal feelings, reactions, or thoughts might you experience from producing quality work?

-
-
-
-
-
-

Appendix D

Rubric with Comment Sections

SELF-REFLECTION RUBRIC				
	4 **Polished Work**	**3** **Just Needs a Little More Work**	**2** **Needs Some More Work**	**1** **Needs Much More Work**
Self-Reflection	Clearly, specifically describes the reason for selecting the entry; a useful suggestion is given for another time.	Clearly describes the reason for selecting the entry; a useful suggestion is given for another time.	I need to describe my reason for selecting the entry more clearly; a suggestion is given for another time.	The reflection is not clear and needs more detail.
Teacher's Comment				
Word Choice	Words are specific and accurately describe what I want to tell; readers would know something about me as a learner.	Most words are specific and describe what I want to tell; readers would know something about me as a learner.	Some words need to be more specific to accurately describe what I want to tell and so readers would know more about me as a learner.	I used simple words such as "good" and "nice." I need to use specific words and more detail so readers will know something about me as a learner.
Teacher's Comment				
Mechanics	Sentences are complete; very few spelling, grammar, or punctuation errors; mistakes do not distract from the content.	Sentences are complete; some minor spelling, grammar, and/or punctuation errors to correct; mistakes do not distract from the content.	Some sentences are run-ons or incomplete; spelling, grammar, and/or punctuation errors distract from the content. I need to proofread my work carefully to correct the mistakes.	My sentences are incomplete and difficult to understand; many errors distract from the content. I need to proofread my work carefully to correct all of the spelling, grammar, and punctuation mistakes.
Teacher's Comment				

Appendix E

Self-Reflection Form with Peer Response

Self-Reflection with Peer Response

Name:_____ Date:_____

Work Sample:_____

This piece of work was difficult in the following ways:

_____

_____

_____

Some things that I did to make this product my best work are:

▸ _____

_____

▸ _____

_____

Signature:_____

Peer Comment: I especially like...

▸ _____

▸ _____

Signature:_____

Appendix F

Working with Others Poster

Working with a Partner or Small Group

Listeners need to remember to:

- Focus attention on the speaker/presenter
- Wait for your turn to talk
- Ask a question or make a comment that shows you listened
- Give the speaker a compliment or describe something that you liked about his/her work
- Show respect by encouraging and supporting the ideas of your partner or others in your group
- Fill out any forms handed out for the activity

Speakers need to remember to:

- Present information in a logical order so that the audience can follow along
- Talk clearly with appropriate volume so your partner or group members can hear
- Keep eye contact with the audience
- Be prepared to answer questions
- Show courteousness by thanking the participant(s) for listening and sharing comments/questions

Appendix G

Reading Portfolio Guide

READING PORTFOLIO

Name: _____	Portfolio Core	_____ / 3
	Portfolio Choice	_____ / 10
Date: _____	Portfolio Presentation	_____ / 5
	Total:	_____ / 18

		Aspect	Criteria	Mark
Portfolio Core	Main Ideas and Events	1.1	Complete all three criteria	/ 3
Portfolio Choice	Related Questions and Activities	1.2	Choose 10 criteria	/ 10
	Main Character	1.3		
	Literary Elements	1.4		
Portfolio Presentation				/ 5
			Total: _____ / 18	

Feedback:

Portfolio Core Guide	Language Arts (Reading Comprehension)
Name: _____ Date: _____ Teacher: _____ 3 Marks: _____ ☆☆☆	Aspect 1.1 **Demonstrate understanding of main ideas and events**

Portfolio Quality = Action + Reflection	Tips to help you create your evidence	

For demonstrating understanding of main ideas and events
 	
 Your portfolio evidence must meet all three criteria.
 	
 ☆ **Criteria #1**
 	
 Select a work sample that demonstrates your ability to understand main ideas and events.
 	
 ☆ **Criteria #2**
 	
 Complete a self-reflection form.
 	
 ☆ **Criteria #3**
 	
 Share your work with a peer.
	Criteria Check			• You must meet all three criteria to receive credit for this aspect.
				
				 • Subject areas to consider include language arts, social studies, and science.
				
				 • Work samples to think about as an entry include the following class activities:
				    • Collecting Details and Main Ideas
				    • Chain of Events
				    • Five W's
				    • E-Chart
				    • Time Line
				    • Spider Map
				    • Venn Diagram
				
				 • A self-reflection form with a peer comment section will be provided.

	Student	**Teacher**	

Format adapted from BC Ministry of Education, 2004, p. 11.

Portfolio Choice Guide	Language Arts (Reading Comprehension)
Name: _____ Date: _____ Teacher: _____ Mark: _____ / 5 ☆☆☆☆☆	Aspect 1.2 **Extend understanding of a given selection by developing related questions and activities**

Portfolio Quality = Action + Reflection				Tips to help you create your evidence
☆☆☆ Generate seven questions based on a reading passage. **Evidence meets three criteria** Two or three must be literal or detail type questions (i.e., answers are found in the text). Two or three need to be inferential type questions (i.e., answers involve using text to read "between the lines"). Two or three should be critical type questions (i.e., answers involve using the text to formulate an opinion or reaction). **Criteria Check** ☐ ☐ ☐	☆ Choose or create an extended activity. **Evidence meets one more criteria** Complete an extended activity suitable for the reading passage. **Criteria Check** ☐	☆ Share your work with a peer. **Evidence meets one more criteria** Share the questions and extended activity with a peer. Complete a self-reflection form. **Criteria Check** ☐	**Mark** / 5	◆ Reading passages can include a story or novel as well as sections or chapters from social studies and science texts. ◆ Refer to the handout for examples of literal, inferential, and critical type question stems. ◆ Choose an extended activity from the list posted in the classroom. Examples of activities include: • creating a new ending • completing a book review • timeline of events • designing a crossword puzzle etc. or ◆ Create your own extended activity such as a board game. ◆ A self-reflection form with a peer comment section will be provided.

Format adapted from BC Ministry of Education, 2004, p. 27.

Portfolio Choice Guide	Language Arts (Reading Comprehension)
Name: _____ Date: _____ Teacher: _____ Mark: _____ / 5 ☆☆☆ ☆☆	Aspect 1.3 **Use graphic forms to summarize and organize information about a main character**

Portfolio Quality = Action + Reflection				Tips to help you create your evidence
☆☆☆ Summarize and organize information about a fictional or non-fictional character. **Evidence meets three criteria** Use a graphic form to list qualities of a main character. Identify at least three key qualities of the character. Provide two pieces of evidence from the text that supports each quality. **Criteria Check** ☐ ☐ ☐	☆ Presenting work. **Evidence meets one more criteria** Present your character description to the class including the key qualities and evidence. **Criteria Check** ☐	☆ Reflect on work. **Evidence meets one more criteria** Complete a self-reflection that includes key strategies you used for locating and summarizing information. **Criteria Check** ☐	**Mark** / 5	◆ Reading passages can include a story or novel as well as sections or chapters from social studies and science texts. ◆ Work samples to think about as entries include the following class activity forms: • Character Sheet & Traits List • Describe a Character • Character Biography • Character Traits • ISP Chart (Information, Sources, Page) ◆ An oral presentation guide is available. ◆ A self-reflection form will be provided.

Format adapted from BC Ministry of Education, 2004, p. 27.

Portfolio Choice Guide	**Language Arts (Reading Comprehension)**
Name: _____	Aspect 1.4
Date: _____	
Teacher: _____	**Identify literary elements**
Mark: _____ / 5 ☆☆☆☆☆	

Portfolio Quality = Action + Reflection				**Tips to help you create your evidence**
☆☆☆ Identify literary elements including setting, plot, and conflict. **Evidence meets three criteria** Describes the setting including where and when. Outlines the plot and climax including the problem/goal, events, and resolution or outcome. Specifies the conflict (i.e., character vs. character, character vs. self, character vs. society, and character vs. nature). **Criteria Check** ▢ ▢ ▢	☆ Compare the story setting to the setting in which you live. **Evidence meets one more criteria** Lists the similarities and differences between the story setting and your own setting. **Criteria Check** ▢	☆ Share your work with a peer. **Evidence meets one more criteria** Share your work with a parent or other adult. Provide the reviewer with a response sheet to fill in. **Criteria Check** ▢	**Mark** / 5	◆ Reading passages can include a story or novel as well as sections or chapters from the social studies text. ◆ Work samples to think about as entries include the following class activities: • Story Maps • History Frame • Setting Comparison • Characters, Problem, Solution • Plot Diagram • Plot Sheet and Conflict List • Problem-Solution chart • Problem & Solution Diagram ◆ The following setting comparison worksheets are available: • Venn Diagram • Setting Comparison • Comparison-Contrast Chart ◆ A self-reflection form with a peer/reviewer comment section will be provided.

Format adapted from BC Ministry of Education, 2004, p. 27.

Appendix H

Scope and Sequence Chart

GRADE LEVEL: K—1	LEARNING OUTCOMES/ STANDARDS
Purpose/ Type ▸ best work ▸ growth	**Grades K to 1 Language Arts** <u>Communicate Ideas and Information</u> (Improving Communications) *It is expected that students will:* • "demonstrate an interest in sharing their work" (BC Ministry of Education, 1996a, p. 24) • "demonstrate appreciation for the work and ideas of others" (p. 24)
Subject(s)/ Curriculum Area(s) ▸ focus on one subject area (reading, writing, math, etc.)	
Audience ▸ parents/family ▸ teacher	<u>Communicate Ideas and Information</u> (Presenting and Valuing) *It is expected that students will:* • "demonstrate pride and satisfaction in using language to express their thoughts, ideas, and feelings " (p. 26)
Criteria ▸ title page ▸ date ▸ self-reflection (guided instruction, one-on-one)	
Selection Process ▸ teacher with a move toward student selections later in the year	<u>Self and Society</u> (Working Together) *It is expected that students will:* • "interact with others" (p. 30) • "speak in turn" (p. 30) • "listen actively, providing verbal and non-verbal responses appropriate to their stages of development and to their cultures" (p. 30)
Time Frame ▸ once per month	
Self-Reflection ▸ novice writers dictate reflections to an adult or a buddy from the higher grade levels ▸ happy face rating scales (e.g., This piece makes me feel…)	
Goal Setting ▸ sentence prompts (e.g., Next time I would like to…)	
Presentation ▸ three-way conference (teacher, parent, student) ▸ portfolio party/tea/evening	
Graduation Program	

GRADE LEVEL: 2	LEARNING OUTCOMES/ STANDARDS
Purpose/ Type ▸ best work and/or growth	**Grades 2 to 3 Language Arts** <u>Communicate Ideas and Information</u> (Presenting and Valuing) *It is expected that students will:* • "demonstrate pride and satisfaction in using language to express thoughts, ideas, and feelings using familiar forms" (BC Ministry of Education, 1996a, p. 48) • "demonstrate a willingness to experiment with communication forms to respond to, inform, and entertain others " (p. 48) • "demonstrate a willingness to participate in a variety of shared activities that include reading and listening to stories and poems, dramatic play, and presenting their own work" (p. 48) <u>Self and Society</u> (Working Together) *It is expected that students will:* • "demonstrate a willingness to communicate a range of feelings and ideas" (p. 52) • "listen actively, responding verbally and non-verbally" (p. 52) • "seek opinions and consider the responses of others" (p. 52) • "demonstrate a willingness to support others by offering compliments and encouragement" (p. 52) **Grade 2 to 3 Personal Planning** <u>The Planning Process</u> *It is expected that students will:* • "describe and use a goal-setting process to set short-term goals" (BC Ministry of Education, 1999, Planning Process section, ¶ 1) • identify progress in achieving their goals and modify goals as necessary (¶ 1)
Subject(s)/ Curriculum Area(s) ▸ one subject area (e.g., reading, writing, mathematics, etc.)	
Audience ▸ teacher ▸ parent/family ▸ peer ▸ buddy	
Criteria ▸ checklist of three to five items (refer to Figure 2) ▸ checklist for portfolio as a whole and self-reflection	
Selection Process ▸ student and teacher	
Time Frame ▸ once a month	
Self-Reflection ▸ "I am selecting this entry for my portfolio because…"; "I am proud of this entry because…"; "This entry is a favourite piece of work because…"; "This piece of work makes me feel…" ▸ Peer Feedback: "I especially like…" (refer to "Mix and Match" in Appendix A)	
Goal Setting ▸ Something that I would do differently next time is…; Something that I still need to work on is… ▸ refer to p. 71 ▸ refer to "Mix and Match" in Appendix A	
Presentation ▸ three-way conference (teacher, parent, student) ▸ portfolio party/tea/evening	
Graduation Program	

GRADE LEVEL: 3	LEARNING OUTCOMES/ STANDARDS
Purpose/ Type ▶ best work and/or growth	**Grades 2 to 3 Language Arts** <u>Communicate Ideas and Information</u> (Presenting and Valuing) *It is expected that students will:* • "demonstrate pride and satisfaction in using language to express thoughts, ideas, and feelings using familiar forms" (BC Ministry of Education, 1996a, p. 48)
Subject(s)/ Curriculum Area(s) ▶ two or three subject areas (reading, writing, math, etc.)	• "demonstrate a willingness to experiment with communication forms to respond to, inform, and entertain others " (p. 48)
Audience ▶ teacher ▶ parent/family ▶ peer ▶ buddy	• "demonstrate a willingness to participate in a variety of shared activities that include reading and listening to stories and poems, dramatic play, and presenting their own work" (p. 48)
Criteria ▶ introduce rubrics for portfolio as a whole and self-reflection (up to four criteria)	<u>Self and Society</u> (Working Together) *It is expected that students will:* • "demonstrate a willingness to communicate a range of feelings and ideas" (p. 52)
Selection Process ▶ student and teacher	• "listen actively, responding verbally and non-verbally" (p. 52) • "seek opinions and consider the responses of others" (p. 52)
Time Frame ▶ every two weeks or monthly	• "demonstrate a willingness to support others by offering compliments and encouragement" (p. 52)
Self-Reflection ▶ sentence prompts (refer to "Mix and Match" in Appendix A)	
Goal Setting ▶ sentence prompts (refer to "Mix and Match" in Appendix A)	**Grade 2 to 3 Personal Planning** <u>The Planning Process</u> *It is expected that students will:* • "describe and use a goal-setting process to set short-term goals" (BC Ministry of Education, 1999, Planning Process section, ¶ 1)
Presentation ▶ three-way conference (teacher, parent, student) ▶ portfolio party/tea/evening	• identify progress in achieving their goals and modify goals as necessary (¶ 1)
Graduation Program	

GRADE LEVEL: 4	LEARNING OUTCOMES/ STANDARDS
Purpose/ Type ▸ best work and/or growth	**Grade 4 Language Arts** Communicate Ideas and Information (Composing and Creating) *It is expected that students will:* • "identify the purpose of and audience for oral, written, and visual communications" (BC Ministry of Education, 1996a, p. 66)
Subject(s)/ Curriculum Area(s) ▸ two or three subject areas (reading, writing, math, etc.)	Communicate Ideas and Information (Presenting and Valuing) *It is expected that students will:*
Audience ▸ teacher and parent/family ▸ a peer or small group ▸ class as a whole ▸ buddies ▸ another class completing portfolios	• "create and express thoughts, ideas, and feelings in a variety of oral, written, and electronic forms" (p. 70) • "create and present a variety of personal and informational communications, including written and oral poems, stories, explanations, informal oral reports and dramas, personal letters, and illustrated charts or posters" (p. 70)
Criteria ▸ rubrics for portfolio as a whole and self-reflection (up to four criteria)	
Selection Process ▸ student and teacher	Self and Society (Working Together) *It is expected that students will:* • "demonstrate respect for others by communicating their ideas and information in an orderly fashion" (p. 74)
Time Frame ▸ every two weeks or monthly	• "listen to and show respect for the ideas of others" (p. 74)
Self-Reflection ▸ sentence prompts (refer to "Mix and Match" in Appendix A)	**Grade 4 Personal Planning** The Planning Process *It is expected that students will:*
Goal Setting ▸ sentence prompts (refer to "Mix and Match" in Appendix A)	• "use a goal-setting process to set short-term and long-term goals" (BC Ministry of Education, 1999, Planning Process section, ¶ 1)
Presentation ▸ three-way conference (teacher, parent, student) ▸ portfolio party/tea/evening	• "explain how various factors influence personal goal achievement" (¶ 1)
Graduation Program	

GRADE LEVEL: 5	LEARNING OUTCOMES/ STANDARDS
Purpose/ Type ▸ best work and/or growth	**Grade 5 Language Arts** Communicate Ideas and Information (Composing and Creating) *It is expected that students will:* • "select and shape information appropriately for specific audiences and purposes" (BC Ministry of Education, 1996a, p. 88)
Subject(s)/ Curriculum Area(s) ▸ three or more subject areas (reading, writing, math, etc.)	Communicate Ideas and Information (Improving Communications) *It is expected that students will:* • "appraise their own and others' work" (p. 90)
Audience ▸ teacher and parent/family ▸ a peer or small group ▸ class as a whole ▸ buddies ▸ another class completing portfolios	Communicate Ideas and Information (Presenting and Valuing) *It is expected that students will:* • "demonstrate pride and satisfaction in using language to create and express thoughts, ideas, and feelings in a variety of oral, written, and electronic forms" (p. 92)
Criteria ▸ rubrics for portfolio as a whole and self-reflection (up to four criteria)	• "create a variety of personal and informational communications, including written and oral stories, poems, or lyrics; explanations and descriptions; informal oral reports and dramatics; and brief factual reports" (p. 92)
Selection Process ▸ student, parent, and teacher	
Time Frame ▸ every two weeks or monthly	Self and Society (Working Together) *It is expected that students will:* • "use the language of praise and constructive feedback when working with others" (p. 96)
Self-Reflection ▸ sentence prompts (refer to "Mix and Match" in Appendix A)	• "listen to and express interest in the ideas of others" (p. 96)
Goal Setting ▸ sentence prompts (refer to "Mix and Match" in Appendix A)	**Grade 5 Personal Planning** The Planning Process *It is expected that students will:* • set personal goals (BC Ministry of Education, 1999, Planning Process section, ¶ 1)
Presentation ▸ three-way conference (teacher, parent, student) ▸ portfolio party/tea/evening	Career Development *It is expected that students will:* • "describe changes in their personal attributes and skills" (BC Ministry of Education, 1999, Career Development section, ¶ 1)
Graduation Program ▸ align one of the subjects with the graduation program format (refer to Tables 4 and 5)	

GRADE LEVEL: 6	LEARNING OUTCOMES/ STANDARDS
Purpose/ Type ▸ best work and/or growth	**Grade 6 Language Arts** <u>Communicate Ideas and Information</u> (Improving Communications) *It is expected that students will:* • "use a given list of criteria to revise their drafts" (BC Ministry of Education, 1996a, p. 112) • "appraise their own and others' work and make suggestions for revision" (p. 112) <u>Communicate Ideas and Information</u> (Presenting and Valuing) *It is expected that students will:* • "demonstrate pride and satisfaction in using language to express their thoughts, ideas, and feelings in various written, oral, visual, and electronic forms" (p. 114) <u>Self and Society</u> (Working Together) *It is expected that students will:* • "use established criteria to evaluate their contributions to the group" (p. 118) **Grade 6 Personal Planning** <u>The Planning Process</u> *It is expected that students will:* • "analyze the factors that could influence personal goals" (BC Ministry of Education, 1999, Planning Process section, ¶ 1) • "outline their progress in meeting short- and long-term goals" (¶ 1) <u>Career Development</u> *It is expected that students will:* "modify and extend their inventories of personal attributes, skills, and successes" (BC Ministry of Education, 1999, Career Development section, ¶ 1)
Subject(s)/ Curriculum Area(s) ▸ three or more subject areas (reading, writing, math, etc.)	
Audience ▸ teacher and parent/family ▸ a peer or small group ▸ class as a whole ▸ buddies ▸ another class completing portfolios ▸ students from a secondary school who are working on graduation portfolios	
Criteria ▸ rubrics for portfolio as a whole and self-reflection (four to six criteria) ▸ student input into establishing criteria	
Selection Process ▸ student, parent, and teacher	
Time Frame ▸ every two weeks or monthly	
Self-Reflection ▸ sentence prompts (refer to "Mix and Match" in Appendix A)	
Goal Setting ▸ sentence prompts (refer to "Mix and Match" in Appendix A)	
Presentation ▸ three-way conference (teacher, parent, student) ▸ portfolio party/tea/evening	
Graduation Program ▸ align two of the subjects with the graduation program format (refer to Tables 4 and 5)	

GRADE LEVEL: 7	LEARNING OUTCOMES/ STANDARDS
Purpose/ Type ▸ best work and/or growth or ▸ Bloom's Taxonomy/Gardener's Multiple Intelligences (refer to Tables 6 and 7) **Subject(s)/ Curriculum Area(s)** ▸ three or more subject areas (reading, writing, math, etc.) **Audience** ▸ teacher and parent/family ▸ a peer or small group ▸ class as a whole ▸ buddies ▸ another class completing portfolios ▸ students from a secondary school who are working on graduation portfolios **Criteria** ▸ rubrics for portfolio as a whole and self-reflection (four to six criteria) ▸ student input into establishing criteria **Selection Process** ▸ student, peer, parent, and teacher **Time Frame** ▸ every two weeks or monthly **Self-Reflection** ▸ sentence prompts (refer to "Mix and Match" in Appendix A) **Goal Setting** ▸ sentence prompts (refer to "Mix and Match" in Appendix A) **Presentation** ▸ three-way conference (teacher, parent, student) ▸ portfolio party/tea/evening **Graduation Program** ▸ two subjects that align with the graduation program format (refer to Tables 4 and 5) ▸ one subject area that aligns with the graduation program format and curriculum area (refer to Table 8)	**Grade 7 Language Arts** Communicate Ideas and Information (Knowledge of Language) *It is expected that students will:* • "adjust the degree of formality in their language to suit the form and purpose of their presentations" (BC Ministry of Education, 1996a, p. 130) • "demonstrate their knowledge of the conventions of public speaking and informal oral presentations" (p. 130) Communicate Ideas and Information (Improving Communications) *It is expected that students will:* • "appraise their own and others' work" (p. 134) Communicate Ideas and Information (Presenting and Valuing) *It is expected that students will:* • "demonstrate pride and satisfaction in using language to create and express their thoughts, ideas, and feelings through a variety of oral, written, and electronic forms" (p. 136) • "create a variety of personal and informational communications, including fiction and non-fiction; written summaries, instructions, and reports; oral and visual presentations; oral and written opinions; poems; or lyrics" (p. 136) • "apply the rules and conventions of formal presentations, including speeches, news reporting, and dramatic monologues" (p. 136) Self and Society (Personal Awareness) *It is expected that students will:* • "formulate communication goals through the identification of personal strengths and areas needing further development" (p. 138) • "create a variety of written and oral communications to record their views, opinions, values, and beliefs" (p. 138) Self and Society (Working Together) *It is expected that students will:* • "elaborate on others' ideas" (p. 140) **Grade 7 Personal Planning** The Planning Process *It is expected that students will:* • "take the steps necessary to carry out their plans" (BC Ministry of Education, 1999, Planning Process section, ¶ 1) • "assess their progress in meeting their" (¶ 1) personal, educational, and career goals • "adjust their goals as necessary in response to change" (¶ 1)

GRADE LEVEL: 8	LEARNING OUTCOMES/ STANDARDS
Purpose/ Type ▸ best work and/or growth or ▸ Bloom's Taxonomy/Gardener's Multiple Intelligences (refer to Tables 6 and 7)	**Grade 8 Language Arts** Communicate Ideas and Information (Knowledge of Language) *It is expected that students will:* • "use grammatically correct language when writing and speaking" (BC Ministry of Education, 1996b, ¶ 13) Communicate Ideas and Information (Composing and Creating) *It is expected that students will:*
Subject(s)/ Curriculum Area(s) ▸ four subject areas	• "formulate pertinent questions to help them develop works of communication on a wide variety of topics" (¶ 16)
Audience ▸ teacher and parent/family ▸ a peer or small group ▸ class as a whole ▸ buddies ▸ another class completing portfolios ▸ students from the senior secondary level who are working on graduation portfolios (e.g., grades 10 – 12)	• "compose or create works of communication for specific audiences and purposes, including to entertain, persuade, or inform" (¶ 16) • "identify the purposes and audiences for their communications" (¶ 16) Communicate Ideas and Information (Improving Communications) *It is expected that students will:* • "appraise and make suggestions for the revision of their own and others' presentations using predetermined and student-developed criteria" (¶ 19)
Criteria ▸ rubrics for portfolio as a whole and self-reflection (up to six criteria) ▸ student input into establishing criteria	• "revise and edit their work to improve content, organization, and effect to best suit their audience and purpose" (¶ 19) • "adjust their form, style, and language for specific audiences and purposes" (¶ 19)
Selection Process ▸ student, peer, parent, and teacher	• "practice, assess, and offer feedback on oral presentations" (¶ 19) Communicate Ideas and Information (Presenting and Valuing)
Time Frame ▸ once a month or term	*It is expected that students will:*
Self-Reflection ▸ sentence prompts (refer to "Mix and Match" in Appendix A)	• "demonstrate pride and satisfaction in using language to create and express their thoughts, ideas, and feelings" (¶ 22) Self and Society (Personal Awareness) *It is expected that students will:*
Goal Setting ▸ sentence prompts (refer to "Mix and Match" in Appendix A)	4. "demonstrate confidence in using language in a variety of formal and informal contexts, both inside and outside the classroom" (¶ 25) Self and Society (Working Together) *It is expected that students will:*
Presentation ▸ three-way conference (teacher, parent, student) ▸ groups/class ▸ portfolio party/tea/evening	• "use various strategies to prompt and support others" (¶ 28) • "evaluate group processes and their own contributions to them by using established criteria" (¶ 28) Self and Society (Building Community) *It is expected that students will:*
Graduation Program ▸ two subjects that align with the graduation program format (refer to Tables 4 and 5) ▸ two subject areas that align with the graduation program format and curriculum area (refer to Table 8)	• "interact purposefully, confidently, and respectfully in a variety of situations" (¶ 31) • "use language to contribute to school celebrations of special events and accomplishments" (¶ 31) **Grade 8 Career and Personal Planning** The Planning Process *It is expected that students will:* • "set short- and long-term educational, career, and personal goals" (BC Ministry of Education, 1997, ¶ 1) • "identify strategies for attaining their short- and long-term goals" (¶ 1) • "evaluate the achievement of their short- and long-term goals" (¶ 1) • "revise their goals as necessary in response to change" (¶ 1)

GRADE LEVEL: 9	LEARNING OUTCOMES/ STANDARDS
Purpose/ Type ▸ best work and/or growth or ▸ Bloom's Taxonomy/Gardener's Multiple Intelligences (refer to Tables 6 and 7)	**Grade 9 Language Arts** Communicate Ideas and Information (Knowledge of Language) *It is expected that students will:* • "use grammatically correct language when writing and speaking" (BC Ministry of Education, 1996b, ¶ 14) Communicate Ideas and Information (Composing and Creating) *It is expected that students will:* • "develop focussed inquiry questions related to concrete or personal topics for specific audiences and purposes" (¶ 17)
Subject(s)/ Curriculum Area(s) ▸ five subject areas	• " use a variety of planning tools and strategies to focus and organize communications for various purposes and audiences " (¶ 17) Communicate Ideas and Information (Improving Communications) *It is expected that students will:*
Audience ▸ teacher and parent/family ▸ a peer or small group ▸ class as a whole ▸ buddies ▸ another class completing portfolios ▸ students from the senior secondary level who are working on graduation portfolios (e.g., grades 10 – 12)	• "appraise their own and others' work to determine the appropriateness of resource choices, language use, and organizational and communication forms" (¶ 20) • "use language that is appropriate to their purpose and audience within the framework of specific guidelines" (¶ 20) • "adjust form, style, and use of language to suit audiences and purposes" (¶ 20) • "monitor their own work for correctness of spelling and punctuation" (¶ 20) Communicate Ideas and Information (Presenting and Valuing) *It is expected that students will:*
Criteria ▸ rubrics for portfolio as a whole and self-reflection (up to six criteria) ▸ student input into establishing criteria	• "demonstrate pride and satisfaction in using language to create and express thoughts, ideas, and feelings in a variety of forms" (¶ 23) • "create a variety of communications designed to persuade, inform, and entertain classroom and other audiences" (¶ 23) • "create a variety of personal, literary, technical, and academic communications" (¶ 23)
Selection Process ▸ student, peer, parent, and teacher	Self and Society (Personal Awareness) *It is expected that students will:*
Time Frame ▸ once a month or term	• "demonstrate confidence in using language in a variety of formal and informal contexts, both inside and outside the classroom" (¶ 26) Self and Society (Working Together) *It is expected that students will:*
Self-Reflection ▸ sentence prompts (refer to "Mix and Match" in Appendix A)	• "use language to prompt and support others" (¶ 29) • "use a variety of ways to express their opinions effectively" (¶ 29) • "evaluate and modify their own roles in group interactions in a variety of contexts" (¶ 29)
Goal Setting ▸ sentence prompts (refer to "Mix and Match" in Appendix A)	Self and Society (Building Community) *It is expected that students will:*
Presentation ▸ three-way conference (teacher, parent, student) ▸ groups/class ▸ portfolio party/tea/evening	• "interact purposefully, confidently, and appropriately in a variety of situations" (¶ 32) • "use language to participate appropriately in celebrations of special events and accomplishments" (¶ 32) **Grade 9 Career and Personal Planning**
Graduation Program ▸ two subjects that align with the graduation program format (refer to Tables 4 and 5) ▸ three subject areas that align with the graduation program format and curriculum area (refer to Table 8)	The Planning Process *It is expected that students will:* • "identify criteria for setting short- and long-term goals" (BC Ministry of Education, 1997, ¶ 2) • "set short-term goals and evaluate long-term goals, revising as necessary" (¶ 2) • "relate their strengths, interests, attributes, and values to their educational, career, and personal goals" (¶ 2) • "develop Student Learning Plans and keep them relevant and up to date" (¶ 2) • "apply study skills and time-management techniques to attain the goals in their Student Learning Plans" (¶ 2) • "revise strategies for achieving goals, in response to change" (¶ 2)

Made in the USA